Behavioural Psychology in Sangam Poetry

Behavioural Psychology in Sangam Poetry

Govindaswamy Rajagopal

Pharos Books

Behavioural Psychology in Sangam Poetry

Govindaswamy Rajagopal
Professor of Tamil
Dept. of Modern Indian Languages and Literary Studies
University of Delhi, Delhi-110007

Email: grajagopaldu@gmail.com
Mobile: 9818487876

Published by
Pharos Books Pvt. Ltd.,
Plot No. 63, First Floor, Pandav Nagar, Delhi-110092

First Published in 2015 with the title
*Mind and Conduct: Behavioural Psychology
in the Sangam Poetry* by
Sun International Publishers,
PG-105, Possangipur, Janakpuri, New Delhi-110058

ISBN: 978-93-67000-44-1   Rs. 150

Dedicated to

Prof. Tamiḻaṇṇal
(Rama. Periya Karuppaṉ)
A fine person, an excellent teacher
and an erudite scholar on Sangam Literature

Contents

Foreword

The book on *Behavioural Psychology in Sangam Poetry* by Dr. Govindaswamy Rajagopal is a commendable effort to look at some aspects of the behaviour dynamics of the dramatis personae. The *tiṇai* worldview of the classical Sangam works propounds an evolutionary and poetic interpretation of "Nature." The three-tiered paradigm of the first elements (*mudaṟporuḷ*), the native and generative elements (*karupporuḷ*) and the appropriate behaviour elements (*uripporuḷ*) is very specific to Tamil culture and literature. The 'Heroic Age' of Tamils standardizes their poetics and hermeneutics against the backdrop of the *akam* and *puṟam tiṇai*s incorporating love in the personal domain and valour in the social sphere.

The study of human behaviour has been the mainstay of all literature all over the world. The body of World classical literature has created archetypes in the early stages of human evolution. Tamil being one of the oldest cultures has created its own literary paradigms which have served as normative standards in literary hermeneutics. Down the centuries, all literary genres have imbibed motifs and themes to expound human behaviour. Behavioural Psychology as an academic discipline is about a century old. It has made great strides in the classification and explanation of human and animal behaviour. Its insights definitely shed light on the multiple themes and sub-themes of the *tiṇai* worldview to understand the behaviour patterns of the classical Sangam poems.

The book aims to understand and explain the important aspects of three kinds of behaviour: Adoptive, Assertive and Aggressive. Against the traditional interpretative framework, the author has made an excellent exercise to revisit a few instances of these behaviour models in the Sangam poems and expand their scope for a behaviouristic understanding. It is a pioneering effort even though a full-fledged study of this kind would invite further research. Even as the Sangam poems lend themselves to multiple interpretations, a behaviouristic perspective would be a clear technique to bring out the multilayered significance of the *uripporuḷ* (behaviour elements) of the *tiṇai*s This volume would serve as a key to open new vistas in the study of human behaviour within Tamil culture and add to the vibrancy of national and international diversity and pluralism of the human communities.

Vanathu Antoni, Ph.D.,
Former Senior Fellow
Deptt. of Modern Indian Languages
and Literary Studies
University of Delhi
Delhi-110007

Preamble

Great literature is known to deal not merely with the pleasant and conscious aspects of the human mind but with the total human psyche, many facets of which are unpleasant and unconscious. Sangam poetry, as acknowledged by several Western scholars, is unsurpassing in world literature. If there is sociological realism in Sangam *puṟam* poems, what is prioritised in Sangam *akam* poems is psychological realism. As D.H. Lawrence has said, "The great relationship for humanity will always be the relation between man and woman. The relation between man and man, woman and woman, parent and child, will always be subsidiary." Sangam *akam* poetry is primarily concerned with the supreme relation between man and woman. Some of the observations made by Wilson Harris provide us with certain fresh insights into Sangam poetry and what may be called *Tiṇai* poetics. He has proposed a unifying theory of life and universe when all could realise the indestructible evanescence of life when all the adversities and oppositions are erased by love and concern.

Describing the Collective Unconscious as the Universal Unconscious, Wilson Harris writes,

> When I speak of the unconscious I am notably speaking of the human unconscious but of the unconscious that resides in objects, in trees, in rivers. I am suggesting that there is a psyche, a mysterious entity that links with the unconscious in nature... In the time-scale of the womb of space all human beings are thus united with the grand scheme of the universe.

Harris, therefore, demands that art makes us think about the unity underlying the humanity, which is known only to our unconscious self. This should be brought to the consciousness of man, the awareness of which will free humanity from all disparities and biases.

Sangam *akam* poetry lends itself readily to the psychological approach, which is an excellent tool for reading beneath the lines and which can afford several profound clues toward solving thematic and symbolic mysteries of a work of art. However, psychological interpretations of time-tested masterpieces have to be carefully handled by qualified scholars. Novices in the field may arrive at incredibly far-fetched conclusions and while seeing a worthy novel or poem as a psychological case study may miss its wider significance and, more tragically, even the aesthetic experience it yields. This is what has happened in the case of several psychological studies of Sangam poems by critics who are ill-acquainted with psychological theories. Not realizing that literary interpretation and psychoanalysis are two different fields, they view Sangam poems solely through the lens of Freud and underestimate their artistic value. But, for this reason, psychoanalysis need not be rejected as neurotic nonsense because it may, in several cases, function as a valuable tool in understanding literature as well as human nature.

Behaviourism is the school of psychology, which attempts to explain behaviour entirely in terms of observable, responses to environmental stimuli. This was introduced in 1913 by J.B. Watson who was influenced by the conditional-reflex experiments of Pavlov. Denying the value of introspection and the concept of consciousness, Watson emphasized laboratory techniques. B.F. Skinner, the modern proponent of Behaviourism, is concerned exclusively with the relationship of observable responses to stimuli and rewards. Metaphysical Behaviourism, Methodological Behaviourism and Analytical Behaviourism are three separate doctrines. To behaviourists, objectively observable organismic behaviour constitutes the only valid scientific basis for psychological data and investigation and stresses the role of the environment as a determinant of human and animal behaviour.

In his *Behavioural Psychology in Sangam Poetry*, Govindaswamy Rajagopal attempts to comprehend the behaviour patterns of the persona in the Sangam poems from the perspective of behavioural psychology. He justifies his interpretation of the poems from the viewpoint of behaviourism on the ground that the *uripporuḷ* of the *tiṇai* framework essentially refers to the feelings, emotions and conduct of the heroine and the hero in the personal and social domains. As he rightly claims, though a few Tamil scholars have analysed the Sangam Corpus from the psychological perspective, very few studies have been made from the standpoint of behaviourism. After giving lucid explanations of all the theories relating to psychology and behavioural psychology, he finds suitable illustrative examples for behavioural psychology in *kaikkiḷai* (unrequited love) and *peruntiṇai* (mismatched love), as well as in all the five kinds (*Kuṟiñci, Mullai, Marutam, Neytal* and *Pālai*) of poems of refined love. Then he passes to poems that depict the adoptive behaviour of the heroes and the heroines, the assertive behaviour of girlfriends and bards, the abnormal behaviour of heroines at the loss of their spouses and subsequently the demonic behaviour of certain kings. Though there is god's plenty, the author has managed to choose the best from the *Akam* anthologies. He has the right secondary sources at his beck and call.

Several *Akam* poems reveal that long before Freud, Jung and their ilk came into being, all the subtle functions of the human mind were fully comprehended by our Sangam poets who could also express them in choice words and measured phrases, employing apt metaphors. Apart from catching the heroine, her confidante, the hero and his friend at the appropriate moment in order to reveal their thoughts and emotions, the Sangam poets made an exemplary use of a character called the foster-mother through whom the feelings and attitudes of a mother may be realistically revealed. The poems in which the foster-mother is reported to speak about her responses to the heroine's romance of courtship or elopement happen to be remarkable psychological studies of the mother of the Sangam Age.

A poem by Veḷḷivītiyār portrays a foster-mother who goes in search of the heroine who has eloped with her lover. She is in search of the missing couple and expresses her disappointment, weariness and frustration when the search proves to be in vain.

> My feet miss their steps; my eyes, tired of looking, have lost their lustre. People in this world other than the couple must certainly be more in numbers than the stars in the wide dark sky (*Kurunto-kai* 44).

In a poem by Mōcikīranār, a foster-mother says how she came to know about the secret love of the heroine.

> When I embraced her, she said that I smelled of sweat. Now I understand why she did not like any hugging—she who is cooler than the white water-lilies growing in the cloud-covered *Potiyil* with the sweet-smelling *vēṅkai* and *kāntaḷ* flowers belonging to Ay of beauteous bracelets (*Kuruntokai* 84).

The foster-mother and mother of a heroine rejoice over the happy life that she has been leading with her husband. The poet Kuṭalūr Kiḻār knows when and how they will express their delight. An exquisite scene from the heroine's kitchen is described by the foster-mother for the benefit of the real mother.

> The bright-browed lady mashes thick curds with her soft *kāntaḷ*-like fingers and wipes them on her clothes. Smoke touches her kohl-lined, *kuvaḷai*-resembling eyes. She was delighted when he enjoyed eating the tamarind curry of a pleasant flavour (*Kurunto-kai* 167).

The poem by Kuḷaṟṟattaṉār presents a foster-mother who consoles the worried mother whose daughter is separated from her husband who has gone on the king's mission.

> Our innocent daughter lives in a small village in a fragrant flower-filled woodland, where cold water-drops dripping from bushes fall on the neck of a jungle fowl attracting the attention of his mate with his calls. The chariot of the great-hearted man who had to travel on a royal assignment will not stay on there (*Kuṟuntokai* 242).

In a poem by Kayamaṉār, we come across a foster-mother who expresses her genuine love and concern for the young lady who has eloped with the lover.

> May there be much of sunless shade and much of well-spread sand on the narrow mountain paths! May there be cool rains in the wasteland which our innocent girl, abandoning us, will be passing by together with the young man bearing a bright, long spear! (*Kuṟuntokai* 378).

In another poem, the same poet pictures a foster-mother as wondering how a young girl who led a carefree life could grow into a bold lady, determined to elope with a young man unmindful of the hardships on the way.

> When she was a child, refusing to drink milk, ignoring her ball, she would play with her friends. Now did she think it easy to go with him on the rugged terrain where a male elephant pokes his lifted tusks into the trunks of an *ōmai* tree and listens to the loud, roaring thunder that reverberates across the mountains scorched by summer heat? (*Kuṟuntokai* 396).

One can go on like this since all the akam poems of the Sangam period are dramatic monologues written by poets who had a superb understanding of the human heart.

Rajagopal's close study of Sangam poems from the standpoint of behaviourism has opened up a fresh area of research. I earnestly hope this will serve the cause of promoting Sangam writings here and abroad.

P. Marudanayagam
Head, Department of Translation
Central Institute of Classical Tamil
Taramani, Chennai-600113

Preface

Tami<u>l</u>, an amazingly accomplished classical language of India, is universally acclaimed for its early literary treasure trove called "Sangam Literature" (*c.* 300 BCE–300 CE). It was my fortune to critically analyse the structure of *mudal* (the "basic elements"), *karu* (the "native elements") and *uri* (the "love themes") in *Akanāṉūṟu* under the guidance of erudite Tamil scholars, **Prof. Tamiḻaṇṇal** (Rama. Periya Karuppan) and **Prof. Pon. Sourirajan** for my doctoral degree. As I have developed a fascination with the vivid and delightful depiction of *akam* ("interior feelings") poems, since 1985 I began studying them earnestly along with critical works on these poems. More than the poems of *puṟam* ("exterior actions"), the *akam* poems have all along been critically viewed and reviewed, analysed and reanalysed, interpreted and reinterpreted from divergent standpoints. Although classical Tamil anthologies were composed in very ancient times, yet they provide ample space for various interpretations. For instance, exceptional research works such as *Treatment of Nature in Sangam Literature* by Prof. M. Varadarajan, *Landscape and Poetry – A Study of Nature in Classical Tamil Poetry* by Xavier Thani Nayagam, *The Tamil Concept of Love in Ahattiṇai* by Prof. V. Sp. Manickam, *Literary Conventions in Akam Poetry* by Kamil Zvelebil, *Tamil Love Poetry and Poetics* by Takanobu Takahashi are worth mentioning here. In the line of divergent studies on *akam* poems, my paper entitled "Birds and Beasts: Codes/ Symbols in the Scheme of Sangam Love Poems" was published (PANDANUS'13, Charles University in Prague, Czech Republic) in the year 2013.

The present study entitled *Behavioural Psychology in Sangam Poetry* is the outcome of the keynote address that I delivered in the workshop on "Sangap Pāḍalgaḷil Naḍattai Uḷaviyal" (Behavioural Psychology in Sangam Poems) sponsored by the Central Institute of Classical Tamil, held at M.D.T. Hindu College, Tirunelveli, Tamil Nadu, on 04th February 2014. The study attempts to trace the emergence and development of the discipline viz. "Psychology" in European countries and also briefly discusses the divergent views of the world-famous Psychologists. Subsequently, aiming at analysing some of the excellent poems of Sangam classics from the psychological perspective, especially within the framework of "Behavioural Psychology," the present research work intends to interpret the appropriate feelings and behaviour patterns of the heroines, and the heroes evoked in *akam* and *pu_ram* poems. As there is space for a new understanding of the traditional concepts, the book earnestly throws light on, how and why, the dramatis personae—*ki_lavan*s (heroes), *ki_latti*s (heroines), *tō_li*s (confidantes), *pāṅgan*s (companions), *pulavar* (poets), *na_rrāy*s (biological mothers), *cevilittāy*s (foster mothers), *parattai*s (concubines), chieftains and kings, and others—behave either with adoptive, or assertive, or aggressive attributes in certain situations. I have earnestly tried to bring out certain fascinating facts of behavioural patterns of the above-mentioned dramatis personae in this book. I believe that the study is an innovative one in terms of interpreting the selected poems in the light of behavioural psychology. Perhaps, the study may be quite an interesting one to the lovers of ancient Tamil literature. I hope this may kindle an interest to look at the entire Sangam literary works altogether from different perspectives to understand their nuanced aesthetic sense of depiction.

Well, in my present endeavour, I would like to thank **Dr. P. Velammal Muthaiah**, former Head of the Department of Tamil, Sri Parasakti College, Courtallam, Tamil Nadu and **Dr. G. Sankara Veerapathiran**, former Associate Professor of Tamil, M.D.T. Hindu College, Tirunelveli, Tamil Nadu, who asked me then to deliver the keynote address on the topic.

I am glad to convey my sincere gratitude to the (late) **Prof. Jaroslav Vacek**, former Director of the Institute of South and Central Asia and former Dean of the Philosophical Faculty, Charles University, Prague, Czech Republic, who suggested me to elaborate the keynote address (then delivered in Tamil) into English in detail. It is because of his constant encouragement that the book has seen the light now.

I owe my earnest thanks to **Prof. Vanathu Antoni** (former Senior Fellow of our Department of Modern Indian Languages and Literary Studies, University of Delhi, Delhi-110007), who has patiently devoted his precious time to enriching the book by sharing his scholarly insights on Psychology and fine-tuning the language of the book. My special thanks to him for rendering a precise "Foreword" to the book.

I wish to convey my gratitude to **Prof. P. Marudanayagam**, Head, Department of Translation, Central Institute of Classical Tamil, Chennai-600113, who willingly has rendered a scholarly "Preamble" to the book amidst his hectic academic assignments.

My sincere thanks to the authorities of the University of Delhi, Delhi-110007 who provided me with the required Financial Aid under the "Scheme of Research and Development Grant 2014–15" which indeed paved the way for its publication in the year 2015. Finally, I would like to thank everyone, including my wife **Dr. Neelakandan Rajeswari** who supported me either directly or indirectly in this endeavour.

01.03.2025 **Govindaswamy Rajagopal**

Abbreviations

ANU   = *Akanāṉūṟu*
Ed.   = Edition
Ibid.   = *Ibidem* (in the same place)
KLT   = *Kalittogai*
KṚT   = *Kuṟuntogai*
NṚI   = *Naṟṟiṇai*
Op. cit. = *Opere citato* (in the work cited)
PA   = *Poruḷ Adigāram*
PNU   = *Puṟanāṉūṟu*
Skt.   = Sanskrit
tr.   = Translation
TKM   = *Tolkāppiyam*

Behavioural Psychology
in Sangam Poetry

Every living being, irrespective of the senses that it possesses, has a typical kind of "behaviour." But the behaviour of a human being is determined by the functions of a "mind." The mind, otherwise known as the "psyche," is not alike or identical to all beings. The conduct of mind differs from being to being, person to person, gender to gender on the basis of "cognizance." Of all beings, humans who possess six senses have the highest knowledge competence or awareness capability called "Cognizance." The "Impulses and Drives" (ID), indeed, play a crucial role in determining their behaviour. "Ego" and "Super Ego" are the other two kinds that determine the behaviour patterns of people, as ably demonstrated by **Sigmund Freud** (1856–1939). The divergent behaviour patterns—originally analysed and duly authenticated in the discipline of "Psychology" between 1850 and 1950—became a fascinating study of the mind and behaviour under the new discipline called "Behaviour Psychology" which flourished after the 1950s. An attempt is made here to understand the behaviour patterns of the dramatis personae in the classical Sangam poems which approximately date back to 300 BCE–300 CE from the perspective of "Behavioural Psychology," a discipline of the modern period. As the *uripporuḷ* ("phase of love") of the *tiṇai* ("landscape") framework essentially refers to the feelings, emotions and behaviours of heroines and heroes in their personal and social domains, there is a justification to interpret the poems from the viewpoint of behaviourism.

Tamiḻ is a classical language of India, spanning over 2000 years and is uniquely known for its early classical literature called *Sanga Ilakkiyam* (Sangam Literature). The term "Sangam," derived from the Pali language, means "gathering, fraternity, academy." In ancient times, Tamil compositions scripted on palm leaves needed to be presented before fellow learned poets of the Tamil Sangams for their suggestions, corrections and final approval before being transformed into manuscripts. According to a legend, three Sangams—with a membership of gods, sages, and kings as poets—existed at different places (Teṉ Madurai, Kabāḍapuram, and Madurai) that lasted for 4,400, 3,700 and 1,850 years respectively. The treasure trove of the third Sangam comprises eighteen literary works viz. *Eṭṭuttogai* (Eight Anthologies) and *Pattuppāṭṭu* (Ten Songs).[1] Composed by over 473 poets, the Sangam classics consist of 2,381 lyrics and 26,350 lines varying in length from 3 to over 800 lines. These poems vividly sketch the love-stricken emotions of gentlewomen as well as the adventurous, dynamic and compassionate conducts of heroic men. Predominantly comprising secular poems, the corpus aesthetically portrays the ever-existing emotions and excitements of human beings under two-fold divisions known as *akam* ("interior feelings") and *puṟam* ("exterior actions").[2]

The *akam* (pronounced *aham*) exquisitely renders the nuances of the interior feelings and behavioural patterns (*uṟi*) of gentlewomen against the backdrop of the native/generative elements (*karu*) of the five landscapes (*mudal*). These behaviours belong to five proper love types viz. *kuṟiñci* (mountainous region – "clandestine meetings"/"union of lovers"), *mullai,* (pastoral/forest region – "wife's hopeful waiting for the arrival of her husband"), *marudam* (agricultural/cultivable region – "sulking of the wife over her husband's unfaithfulness"), *neydal* (seashore region – "anxious waiting of the beloved"/"wife for the arrival of her lover"/"husband who fails to return at the agreed time") and *pālai* (desert/parched wasteland region – "the lover's/husband's departure to an alien country through the wilderness in search of wealth or in the quest of joining the army to wage war or for gaining knowledge"). Besides these five appropriate love types, there are two types of "inferior love" known as *kaikkiḷai*[3] ("one-sided affair" or "unrequited love") and *peruntiṇai*[4] ("mismatched love" or "excessive lust") that very rarely get represented in the classics of Sangam anthologies. At one end, *peruntiṇai* or the major type refers to the man-woman relationship which is forced and loveless. A man and a woman, mismatched in age, come together for duty, convenience, or lust. At the other extreme is *kaikkiḷai* (literally, the "base relationship") which refers to the one-sided affair, unrequited love, or desire inflicted on an immature girl who does not understand it. Neither of these extremes is the proper subject of *akam* poetry. "They are common, abnormal, undignified, fit only for servants" (Ramanujan 1985:236) as per *Tolkāppiyam* (*c.* 300 BCE), the earliest extant Tamil grammatical treatise.

Arguably, corresponding to the aforesaid love themes, the *puṟam* intensely depicts the fearless, dynamic, and generous behaviours of heroic men under the themes viz. *veṭci* (cattle raids/cattle lifting from a neighbouring country), *vañci* (invasion of a neighbouring country), *uḷiñai* (besieging and capturing fort), *tumbai* (waging a war), *vāgai* (celebrating the victory of war), *pāḍāṇ* (praising the valour or munificent of a chieftain/a king) and *kāñci* (illustrating the impermanence of life).

Being composed roughly between 300 BCE and 300 CE, the Sangam literary works have been critically analysed and re-analysed from such divergent perspectives as literature, linguistics, history, sociology, philosophy, psychology, anthropology, culture, and so on. Any text, if it is interpreted time and again by divergent and sometimes conflicting viewpoints at different periods in history, becomes entitled to higher recognition and appreciation and it can be truly and duly called a "world-class masterpiece." Although the Tamil̤ classical anthologies are composed in very ancient times, yet they provide more space for various interpretations. Evidently, such studies testify to the uniqueness and the greatness of the classical Tamil̤ literary works and as such they are universally recognised by litterateurs of eminence and scholars of repute of the modern and post-modern periods. Some research studies including *The Psychological Symbolism of Pālai in Kur̤untogai* (1971) by Lalitha Sambamoorthy and *Sanga Ilakkiyattil Ul̤aviyal* (Psychology in Sangam Literature), (1994) by D. Sivaraj analysed the ancient Tamil̤ poems from the psychological perspective,[5] yet no study has been made on the Sangam classics specifically from the standpoint of "Behavioural Psychology." Hence, the present research work intends to study and interpret some of the classical poems from a behaviouristic standpoint. The application of the principles of a modern discipline like behavioural psychology to interpret the poems of a bygone era may raise questions of methodology. Justification for such an undertaking lies in the fact that the *uripporul̤* of the *tiṇai* scheme precisely refers to the appropriate feelings and behaviour patterns of the heroines and the heroes. Besides the whole of the evolutionary history of humans is nothing but their adoptive and adaptative behaviours to the environment. When classical literature like Sangam poems prescribes appropriate personal and social behaviours as normative in the composition of the poems, a behaviouristic analysis of the poems gains in acceptability and receptivity. Hence, there is a space for a new understanding of traditional concepts.

Psychology and Psychologists

Psychology[6] is the scientific study of mental functions and behaviours of human beings and animals. The word *Psychology* literally means the "Study of the Soul" (*psyche* meaning "breath" in Greek, "spirit," or "soul"; and − *logos*, translated as "study," "science" or "research"). "*Psyche* means "the mind"; "the mental life" including both conscious and subconscious processes" (Pandya 2013:9). The Latin word *psychologia* was first used by the Croatian humanist and Latinist **Marko Marulić** in his book, *Psichiologia de ratione animae humanae* in the late 15th century or early 16th century. The earliest known reference to the word *psychology* in English is by **Steven Blankaart** in 1694 in *The Physical Dictionary* referring to "Anatomy," which treats of the Body, and Psychology, which treats of the Soul.[7] In the quest to study the mental functions of human beings, one needs to analyse their thoughts, consciousness, dreams, intuitions, faith, etc.

The study of psychology in a philosophical context dates to the ancient civilizations of Egypt, Greece, China, India, and Persia. Historians point to the writings of ancient Greek philosophers viz. Thales, Plato, and Aristotle (especially in his *De Anima* treatise, "Aristotle's Psychology," *Stanford Encyclopedia of Philosophy*) as the first significant body of work in the West to be rich in psychological thought.[8] As early as the 4th century BC, Greek physician **Hippocrates** theorizes that mental disorders are of a physical, rather than divine, nature.[9]

German physician **Wilhelm Maximilian Wundt** (1832–1920) is credited with introducing psychological discovery into a laboratory setting. Known as the "Father of Experimental Psychology," he founded the first psychological laboratory at Leipzig University in 1879. Wundt focuses on breaking down mental processes into the most basic components, motivated in part by an analogy to recent advances in chemistry, and its successful investigation of the elements and structure of material. Although Wundt, himself, is not a structuralist, his student **Edward Bradford Titchener** (1867–1927), a major figure in early American Psychology, is a structuralist thinker opposed to functionalist approaches.[10]

"Functionalism" forms as a reaction to the theories of the structuralist school of thought and is heavily influenced by the work of the American philosopher, scientist, and psychologist **Willian James** (1842–1910). James feels that psychology should have practical value and that psychologists should find out how the mind can function to a person's benefit. In his book, *Principles of Psychology*, published in 1890, he lays the foundations for many of the questions that psychologists would explore for years to come. Other major functionalist thinkers include **John Dewey** (1859–1952) and **Harvey A. Carr** (1873–1954).[11]

Other 19th-century contributors to the field include the German psychologist **Hermann Ebbinghaus** (1850–1909), a pioneer in the experimental study of memory, who developed quantitative models of learning and forgetting at the University of Berlin, and the Russian-Soviet physiologist **Ivan Pavlov** (1849–1936), who discovers in dogs a learning process that is later termed "classical conditioning" and applied to human beings.[12] Starting in the 1950s, the experimental techniques developed by Wundt, James, Ebbinghaus, and others re-emerge as experimental psychology and become increasingly cognitivist—concerned with information and its processing—and, eventually, constituting a part of the wider cognitive science.[13] In its early years, this development is seen as a "revolution" as cognitive science both responded to and reacted against then-popular theories, including psychoanalytic and behaviourist theories.

Behavioural Psychology and Behaviourists

"Behavioural Psychology," otherwise known as "Behaviourism," is a branch of Psychology that emerges later focusing on observable behaviours. It is the study of behaviour patterns as to why human beings think and behave in certain ways. Human behaviour includes many factors like thinking, feeling, writing, reading, imagining and acting, almost everything that a person does. It is a perspective that has become a predominant area of interest during the early decades of the 20th century. The basis of Behavioural Psychology suggests that all behaviours of human beings are learned. Analyzing the cognition, attention, emotion, phenomenology, motivation, brain functioning, personality, behaviour and interpersonal relationships of human beings by applying the principles of perception and conception are what could be called "Behavioural Psychology."

Significantly shifting from the methodologies and analyses adopted by Wundt, James and others the Austrian physician **Sigmund Freud** (1856–1939) developed psychoanalysis which comprises a method of investigating the mind and interpreting experience; a systematized set of theories about human behaviour; and a form of psychotherapy to treat psychological or emotional distress, especially unconscious conflict. Freud's psychoanalytic theory is largely based on interpretive methods, introspection and clinical observations. It becomes very well known, largely because it tackles subjects such as sexuality, repression, and the unconscious mind as general aspects of psychological development. Clinically, Freud helps pioneer the method of free association and a therapeutic interest in dream interpretation.[14]

He classifies human behaviours according to a person's awareness: **(a) Conscious Behaviour**: Any behaviour that the person is aware of (e.g., walking, eating, speaking, etc.), and **(b) Unconscious Behaviour**: Any behaviour that the person is not aware of (e.g., mannerisms, shaking of the legs while sitting, biting fingers, etc.). He categorizes the human mind as possessed of three layers viz. **Conscious Mind**, **Subconscious Mind** and **Unconscious Mind**. According to him, the Unconscious Mind is bigger than the Conscious Mind. The Conscious Mind is the base of our cognizance and emotions. One could locate its presence in the psyche. The Subconscious Mind is positioned a little deeper than the Conscious Mind. It is a part of the former yet a little away from our cognizance and memory. When we try with a little effort, we can bring the things (lying in it) to the sphere of our cognizance. Whereas the Unconscious Mind—which functions as the huge reservoir of our thoughts, emotions, passions, desires and memories—is beyond the ken of our perception. Bitter episodes, painful experiences, occurrences filled with tensions and contradictions and similar things get stored in the aforesaid reservoir. Our suppressed feelings, passions and memories which evolve allegedly out of social rejection, would get deposited in our Unconscious Mind. Without our awareness/knowledge, the Unconscious Mind naturally would affect our behaviours and experiences, thus observes Freud.[15]

While explaining the aforesaid three layers of the mind, Freud classifies the functions of the mind into three categories. They are: **ID, Ego** and **Super Ego. ID** is the abbreviated form of "Impulses and Drives,"[16] the unconscious part of the psyche, or mind which gives free rein to drives and impulses based on instinct, which induce human beings/animals to behave in certain ways. IDs are filled with the power of libido viz. the basic instincts called "sexual feelings." IDs function on the principles of pleasure, seeking whole enjoyment in everything at any cost. As such, they do not care for any ethical values viz. good, bad, virtue, vice, etc. These traits, indeed, are part of the Unconscious Mind. Ego, a term in Psychology, as such does not mean 'pride' or 'arrogance' as we usually interpret it at present. Rather it has positive attributes. Understanding the realities of practical life, Ego accordingly modifies/alters the evil nature of ID, and it ably handles transactions with the external world. By suppressing/ concealing the Unconscious Mind, Ego rules over ID through the rationality of the Subconscious Mind. It functions willfully by adhering to the principles of Realism. The Ego is responsible for shaping the human personality with attributes such as cognizance, self-shielding, performing skill, experimenting, planning, executing, etc. It makes us understand the self and the world by sheer regulation of thoughts. When the ID and the external actions of society function in opposite directions, it is the Ego that gets more strained in keeping them balanced. The tendency of the mind to idealize great personalities like parents, teachers and other super role models in life and behave with noble traits is called "Super Ego." It is "the moral aspect of personality, developed on the basis of conditioning by parents during childhood, which upholds values and ideals and is constantly in conflict with the *id*" (Pandya, *Ibid.*, p. 55). This is the tendency of the mind in which thoughts and actions are urged to be fully absorbed by superb attributes. It is the Super Ego that completely censures ID whenever evil feelings and wicked thoughts arise in a person's psyche. It is otherwise called "Conscience." It is our conscience which displays guilty feelings. The aforesaid three categories, in fact, are the hierarchical sectors of the mind in ascending order. They denote respectively a person possessed of animalistic attributes, a good man of astuteness and a great social human being who cares for others' welfare.

By the end of the 20th century, the Psychology departments in American universities become scientifically oriented. As a result, they marginalize Freudian theory and dismiss it as a "desiccated and dead" historical artefact.[17] Contradicting the psychoanalytic theory of Freud, psychologists like **Hans Jurgen Eysenck** (1916–1997) and behavioural psychologists like **John Broadus Watson** (1878–1958), **Burrhus Frederic Skinner** (1904–1990) and others propound a different theory to understand human behaviour. "It is the environment, in which a person grows, ostensibly determines his/her behaviour and personality," thus they observe. "Besides the person's inborn attributes of body and mind, it is, in fact, the environment that plays the significant role in shaping one's character and conduct," so they elaborate.

"Carl Jung, a Swiss psychiatrist, worked with Freud and later formed his own school of psychoanalysis. According to Jung's complex and rather mystical theory of personality, there are two levels in the unconscious. The *personal unconscious* contains experiences of the individual which have been repressed or forgotten. The *collective unconscious*, common to all of us, contains behaviour patterns and memories derived from our ancestral past. Jung also grouped individuals as introverts and extroverts, a distinction later adopted and modified by other theorists," (*Ibid.*, p. 56). As Behaviourism became the dominant school of thought during the 1950s, John B. Watson established the discipline of "Behavioural Psychology" for the first time in the early 20th century. Later **Edward Thorndike** (1874–1949), **Clark Leonard Hull** (1884–1952), **Edward Chace Tolman** (1886–1959), **B.F. Skinner** (1904–1990) and others embraced and extended the discipline as well-oriented and resourceful by their sheer contribution. Theories of learning put forward by them emphasized the ways in which people might be predisposed or conditioned by their environments to behave in certain ways. Classical conditioning is an early behaviourist model. "For the present, though, the consensus holds that each individual creates his own environment. He picks and chooses from a range of stimuli and events largely on the basis of his genetic inheritance and creates a unique set of experiences," (*Ibid.*, p. 7). It posits that behavioural tendencies are determined by immediate associations between various environmental stimuli and the degree of pleasure that follows. Behavioural patterns, then, are understood to consist of the organisms' conditioned responses to the stimuli in their environment. The stimuli are held to exert influence in proportion to their repetition or to the previous intensity of their associated pain or pleasure.

B.F. Skinner's Behaviourism believes that the contents of the mind are not open to scientific scrutiny and that scientific psychology should emphasize the study of observable behaviour. 'Skinner sees human behaviour as determined largely by its consequences. If rewarded, behaviour is repeated; if punished, it is avoided. This is in line with the findings of Ivan Pavlov when he studied conditional reflexes' (*Ibid.*, p. 58). He focuses on behaviour—environment relationship and analyzes overt[18] and covert[19] (i.e., private) behaviour as a function of the organism interacting with its environment.[20] Behaviourists usually reject or deemphasize dualistic explanations such as "Mind" or "Consciousness," and, in lieu of probing an "Unconscious Mind" that underlines unawareness, they speak of the "contingency-shaped behaviours" in which unawareness becomes outwardly manifest.[21] "Whilst the mind exists within the brain, it is not a physical thing and has no particular location," thus states Pandya (*Ibid.,* p. 10).

Behavioural Patterns

Human behaviour is based on several attributes inherited genetically before the actual birth. "Chief among these is the structure and function of the brain, our inborn reflexes and instincts. Our responses are modified, as we develop, by lessons we learn and examples we choose to follow or avoid. These lessons, in turn, are based on our perceptions. Behaviour is also modulated by a host of other factors which include the environment, positive or negative reinforcement, the state of mind at a given moment and the use or abuse of chemicals (including nicotine, caffeine, and alcohol)," thus further states Pandya (*Ibid.,* pp. x–xi). Evidently, behavioural patterns of human beings can be classified broadly under the two-fold categories of **Normal Behaviour** and **Abnormal Behaviour**. In other words, they can be categorized as **Usual Behaviour** and **Unusual Behaviour** or as **Acceptable Behaviour** and **Unacceptable Behaviour**. In another sense, they can be branded under the terms of **Adoptive/Adjusting Beha-**

viour and **Objecting/Rejecting Behaviour**. The positive behavioural patterns like living in harmony with others, making others comply with them and so on can be termed as "Adoptive/Adjusing Behaviour." The negative behavioural patterns like getting angry, becoming furious, disrupting and destroying others' sentiments, either verbally or physically can be termed as "Objecting/Rejecting Behaviour."

In the cultural milieu of India, it is mostly the females who earnestly behave as the people of "adoptive/adjusting." In fact, they have been moulded to adjust with their counterparts by sacrificing their comforts for the sake of family/society. On the contrary, the males in general, behave as the category of "objecting or rejecting" only to enjoy the life at the cost of their counterparts. Their own distinctive "impulses and drives" (ID) become the basis and root cause for the aforesaid behavioural patterns of the two genders.

It is due to the friction and confrontation which exist ever between the "mind" and "body" or the "heart" and "body" called "interior" and "exterior"; the "home" and "house" called the "inner world" and "outer world" that the "impulses and drives" of male and female remain juxtaposed to each other. In fact, the conflicting "ID" are the sole cause for the females to become more emotional and compliant while the males become dominant and dictating. It is on this basis that women function as the gender of **home making cum home keeping** whereas men as that of the **house managing cum house guarding**. While women take care of "home making" i.e., organizing and safeguarding the structure of society, generally men sabotage the structure by their bad habits, and thereby they are branded "home breakers." A quite number of men, in one way or other, do have one or many bad habits like addiction to alcohol or drugs, smoking *beedi*, cigarette etc., chewing *pān-parāg, guṭka* etc., (tobacco mixed with some chemicals for intoxication), inhaling *ganja* (marijuana) and hero-in, gambling, playing cards, keeping extra-marital relationship and so on. These harmful habits, needless to say, as we witness, destroy the matrix of the family and the societal structure as well.

Human beings can be classified into the following three categories on the basis of their behavior:

People of Adoptive Behaviour
People of Assertive Behaviour
People of Aggressive Behaviour

People of "adoptive behaviour" are those who behave with a spirit of adjustment and are flexible with others in all situations. They may also be otherwise called people of "passive behaviour." They do not make any demands, or ask for what they want, keep anger inside, say "sorry" frequently and say "yes" when they want to say "no." They do not rule over and dominate others in any manner. In a nutshell, they are fine/nice personalities. People of "assertive behaviour" are those who usually selfless, astute and unemotional. They are great personalities and noble ones in every sense. They are the people who are honest and brave and are very clear about what they want.

People of "aggressive behaviour" are those who possess a strong physique, and dynamic mental power, and are extremely confident in their strengths. They are indeed ever ready to face any challenge or fight without hesitation. Simply they could be termed as "hotheads"—generally possessing the attributes of shouting, bullying, bossing, showing off, and intimidating nature.

The heroes and heroines of fine qualities depicted in the classical poems of Sangam anthologies could be said to possess "adoptive behaviour." While *tōḻi* (Skt. *sakhi* i.e., the female companion of heroine) and poets/bards/minstrels manifest "assertive behaviour," the dynamic warriors and great kings exhibit "aggressive behaviour" through their attributes and personalities.

Behavioural Psychology in Sangam Poetry

As stated elsewhere, *akam* and *puṛam*, the two-fold divisions of Sangam poems, essentially refer to the "inner feelings" and "outer actions" of women and men respectively. The two-fold themes of ancient Tamiḻ poems signify the concept of binary opposition such as "inner" *vs.* "outer," "self" *vs.* "other," "nature" *vs.* "culture," and "household" *vs.* "wilderness" (Ramanujan, *Op. cit.*, p. 263). The conception, being part of the form as well as the content of *akam* and *puṛam* poems, indeed, represents two contrasting realms of women and men respectively. Women generally having soft, gentle, tender, caring, warm and kind behaviours, naturally qualify to be identified as the representatives of *akam*. Whereas men commonly being strong, hard, tough, determined, and business-oriented, obviously qualify to be identified as the representatives of *puṛam* as envisaged in the literary conventions of the ancient Tamiḻ poems. Through all their "inner feelings,"[22] women, in fact, strive hard to build up a family system and earnestly try to sustain it at any cost. On the contrary, through their "exterior actions," men indeed attempt essentially to manage the household with the resources of money and materials and of course, sincerely try to protect the kingdom by joining the army.

The mind plays an important role both in the inner feelings and in the external actions of people. It is to be remembered here that the term Psychology refers to the scientific study of psyche/ mind/heart or soul. The mind (*man* in Skt. > *maṉam* in Tamiḻ) as such functions as per the directions of cerebral propensity or mental capability. It is observed that there exists a close connection between the "love feelings of heart/psyche/soul" and the secretion of the hormone called "Oxytocin." Psychologists term the change in the behaviour of a person due to the stimulus of oxytocin hormone as "the feeling of love."[23] "Love" (*kādal* in Tamiḻ), an extended and nuanced feeling of lust, is consummated in the enjoyment of sexual pleasure. "Love" is inclusive of the basic instinct called "lust." But the "lust" is devoid of "love."

When the feeling of love emerges quite naturally among adults without any encouragement or persuasion from anyone, it is considered normal. The feeling of love has dimensions named after *kuriñci, mullai, marudam, neydal* and *pālai*, based on their varying moods. But if love/lust feelings arise only in the male psyche, then they are branded as *kaikkiḷai* ("one-sided affair" or "unrequited love") and *peruntiṇai* ("excessive love" or "mismatched love") based on dismal emotions. Only *Kalittogai* (herein after *KLT*), a unique anthology of Sangam classics, comprises poems depicting both the aforesaid dismal feelings so aesthetically.

Behavioural Psychology in *Kaikkiḷai* (Unrequited Love)

Tolkāppiyam[24] (*c.* 300 BCE), the oldest Tamil work on grammar and poetics, does not subscribe to *kaikkiḷai* and *peruntiṇai* as appropriate love feelings of well-matched lovers.[25] However, it strangely assigns them to the first and last positions in the scheme of *akam* poetry in which the appropriate "five love types" (*kuriñci, mullai, marudam, neydal* and *pālai*) are placed in between. Tolkāppiyar, the author of the grammatical work assigns these atypical love feelings as only fit for servants or workmen since they do not have the necessary strength of character (Akattiṇai Iyal 25–26). Since the people of prominence dwell in the "center" and the service class in the "peripheries," perhaps the grammarian places the inappropriate love feelings such as *kaikkiḷai* and *peruntiṇai* respectively in the first and last positions, keeping the appropriate love feelings in the middle. The role of the environment in determining the uncharacteristic behavioural patterns of the service classes is to be understood as they ponder over grimy and hopeless conditions. While the grammarian duly assigns the *mudal poruḷ* (the "first things" or the "basic things" i.e., the region, season and hour), *karupporuḷ* elements (the "native" or generative elements" or the "objects of environment" such as flora and fauna, presiding deity, people and their profession, etc.) besides the "subject matter of love themes" called *uripporuḷ* (the "human feelings" appropriately set in *mudal* and *karu*) to "the middle five love categories," he does not assign the first two elements (*mudal* and *karu*) to *kaikkiḷai* and *peruntiṇai* as these love themes are abnormal, abject and unusual to be found only with the people of the service class anywhere and at any time.

In *akam* literary convention, it is only the hero who is portrayed indulging in such inappropriate aspects of love. **No woman character is portrayed in any of the ancient Tamiḻ literary texts indulging in such unrequited/excessive love.** Though "the basic instinct"/"sexual feeling" is common to both sexes, it is only the males (not all), who more often violate the norms and culture of society. Their masculinity filled with manliness, excessive passion and self-appeasing and uncaring tendency apparently pushes them to indulge in such an odd rather obnoxious manner. Whereas women—the guardians of social norms and culture—known for shyness, modesty, kindness and self-sacrifice, usually never indulge in such disgraceful activities. This is what gets reflected in the early Tamiḻ poems too.

While defining the *kaikkiḷai*, the *Tolkāppiyam* (Akattiṇai Iyal 50) outlines the following aspects: "The hero approaches a girl who is not emotionally mature enough to respond to his inflicting and incurable passion of love; tries to strike a conversation with her describing his distress and her indifference but does not get any response and yet indulges himself in a such a talk" (Manavalan 2007:35). To illustrate the aforesaid categories of unrequited love, there are not many examples found in classical

Tamiḻ literature. However, here is one from *Kuṟuntogai* (herein after *KṞT*).[26] The *akam* convention, as outlined in the *Tolkāppiyam*, puts forth the notion that any matter related to love and family making involving the hero and the heroine (the clandestine meeting, union, separation, elopement, wedding, sulking over infidelity, etc.) should always take place only through *tōḻi*, the confidante/girlfriend of the latter. So, a hero in *Kuṟuntogai* anthology requests the *tōḻi* to arrange for a meeting with his beloved. However, perhaps doubting his intention or weighing his integrity, she has not paid due attention to his request. Perturbed over her non-cooperative attitude, the hero reveals his disturbed mind and anxious thoughts to her in the following poem.

> One is desperate
> to ride a palm-stem horse,
> to wear a wreath of
> milkweed buds
> and be a laughing stock
> of the marketplace.
> One is out for any shame
> when the blinding passion of love
> overwhelms the heart.
>
> (Pēreyiṉ Muṟuvalār, *Kuṟuntogai* 17,
>   tr. Thangappa 2010:6)

Here in the poem, we can see how the enraged mind of the hero tosses him over his failed mission. Obsessed with the desire to see his beloved and thereby for physical union with her, he is in a desperate mood and throws his senses into the wind. As such, passion/obsession/addiction always forsakes rationality. So, he utters, rather threatens that he would go even to the extent of riding a 'palmyra stem horse.' When he rides the dried-up palmyra stem (made as a horse and pulled by village boys), eventually there would be bleeding profusely from his thigh and in the course of action, he would meet with death soon. As the reeking cones of *erukkam* (milkweed) buds are ceremonially draped over the dead bodies, the hero uttering the same—wearing them as flowers on his head—suggestively means that soon he would embrace the death. The disgraceful act would certainly make him a laughingstock in the eyes of the public. Besides it would bring dishonour to his family as well as to his beloved. Also, it would see him dead at the end, if people did not stop him immediately. This shameful and senseless act is the outcome of abnormality stimulated by his obsession with sex. Obviously, it is because of the passionate sexual urge, numerous lives have been lost on the planet since time immemorial. It is, in a way, similar to that of addiction to alcoholism by which only the menfolk become the losers. The irony is that the women folk, the so-called "weaker sex" are, in fact, stronger than their counterparts. Not only do they stay away from such addictions but also overcome challenges by sustaining pulls and pressures from others. Hence, the *tōḻi,* neither acts to the earlier request nor reacts to the latter threat from the hero. She is poised and gentle and so keeps mum. Moreover, there is no response from the heroine in this regard. Suffice it to say that "men are physically strong but mentally weak," at least, in the affairs of the heart.

When a man becomes infatuated with a woman, especially smitten by her beauty, he lands as a crazy person or a kind of madman. Subsequently, his lovesickness drives him to go behind her wherever she goes. It urges him to utter whatever comes to his mind. Besides, it forces him to behave strangely rather awkwardly with no feeling of shame or shyness only to attract her. As he is concerned wholly with satiating his sexual desire, he forgets the reality. Invariably, he becomes a laughingstock to everyone and ironically to the woman whom he is stalking as well. Here is a poem from *Kalittogai*, sketching the obsession of a lover so aes-thetically.[27]

"O your hair," he said,
"it's like rainclouds
moving between
branches of lightening.
It parts five ways
between gold ornaments,
braided with a length of flowers
and the fragrant screwpine.

"O your smiles, your glistening teeth,
words sheer honey,
mouth red as coral,
O fair brow,
I want to tell you
something,
listen, stop and listen,"

he said, and stopped me.

Came close,
to look closer
at my brow, my hands, my eyes,
my walk, my speech,
and said, searching
for metaphors:

> "Amazed, it grows small, but it isn't the crescent.
> Unspotted, it isn't the moon.
> Like bamboo, yet it isn't on a hill.
> Lotuses, yet there's no pool.
> Walk mincing, yet no peacock.
> The words languish, yet you're not a parrot,"

> and so on.

> On and on he praised my parts
> with words gentle and sly,
> looked for my weakening
> like a man with a net
> stalking an animal,

> watched me
> as my heart melted,

> stared at me
> like a butcher at his prey,
>
> O he saluted me, saluted me,
> touched me, O he touched me,
> a senseless lusting elephant
> no goad could hold back.
>
> Salute and touch,
> and touch again he did,
> but believe me, friend,
> I still think he is not really
>
> a fool by nature.

> (Kabilar, *Kalittogai* 55,
> tr. Ramanujan 1985:197–198)

The craziness of the fall-guy who blabbers like a possessed man with rhetorical words is seen here. He eulogizes the physical beauty of the girl—her black tresses, fair brow, glistening teeth, reddened mouth, soft words, tender shoulder, blossomed breasts, excellent gait and whatnot—alas to the woman who does not show any interest in him. In addition to babbling, he behaves quite disdainfully stalking her untiringly and saluting her frequently. But after all his efforts, the woman is not moved even a bit but feels sad for his silly behaviour. Though the girl is mature enough to understand his advanced sexual feelings, she shows no response. Her stoic calmness, a sense of modesty, depicted here is contrary to the immature love feelings of the man. As men largely approach their counterparts as objects of sex, the hero of the poem too evidently behaves in a similar fashion. Of course, women too become attracted to their counterparts at some point in time or other. But normally they restrain themselves from showing their feelings overtly in the interest of protecting their honour as well as that of their family. Essentially, their concern is not centered on self-gratification but towards a worthy "family making" which is juxtaposed to the behaviour of their counterparts.

Behavioural Psychology in *Peruntiṇai* (Mismatched Love)

Another inappropriate love type, more awful than *kaikkiḷai*, is known as *peruntiṇai*, the seventh and the last category in the scheme of *akam* poetry. While defining the *peruntiṇai*, the *Tolkāppiyam* (Akattiṇai Iyal 51) outlines the following four aspects: "The act of mounting the horse made of palm stems; being in a state of past youth; being head over heels in lust beyond control; and forcefully taking a nonchalant lady owing to his overflowing passion" (Manavalan, *Op. cit.*, p. 37). "Of the four, the aspects of mounting the palmyra-horse and that of forcefully taking a lady are ascribed only to the hero. The other two are common to both lovers. **Tamiḻ tradition does not depict a lady in love as mounting the palm-horse**. In the case of the hero too, it is rarely resorted to. When the parents of the lady love refuse to give her in marriage, the hero resorts to mounting the palm-horse to declare his premarital clandestine love to the public with a view to forcing them to agree to their marriage" (*Ibid.*).

Again, in the present category too, it is only the hero who is portrayed as indulging in such an inappropriate aspect of love. The women, as stated elsewhere, the guardians of social norms and culture—known for their gentle attributes—normally never indulge in the aforesaid disgraceful actions. A woman does not see herself or anyone else as damaging her reputation. She is more conscious about her image i.e., modesty. But on the contrary, man does not mind bringing his private matters to the public domain aiming at his self-interest. In *akam* convention, when the hero is spurned either by the heroine or by her family members, he climbs a 'palmyra stem'/'frond horse.' The palmyra stem would be drawn through the streets of the town. He wears *erukkam* (milkweed) flower garlands and carries a picture of his lover. People in the streets, seeing him in a pathetic condition, laugh. And he suffers the ridicule of the town people also. This is the drastic move by the hero to get the attention of his beloved or her family. The hero takes this extreme step when all else fails. This sort of 'abnormal behaviour' is seemingly depicted in *Kuṟuntogai* strangely in *kuṟiñci* (sexual union) love theme that too in a poem penned down by a woman poet Aḷḷūr Naṉmullaiyār. The following poem[28] shows how and why a hero annoyed over the unconcerned attitude of the heroine and or her family members, contemplates to ride a 'palmyra stem'/'frond horse.'

> Those who are aware of mornings,
> daytimes, helpless evenings, nights when
> the town sleeps and dawn hours, do not,
> have true love.
>
> If I climb on a palmyra stem horse and
> ride on the streets, people will see clearly
> and there will be accuse and blame.
>
> Living is painful; separation is also painful.
>
> (Aḷḷūr Naṉmullaiyār, *Kuṟuntogai* 32,
> tr. Vaidehi Herbert)[29]

In enacting such love themes of *peruntiṇai*, as in the case of *kaikkiḷai*, servants and workmen are portrayed with grey shades. Physically challenged people (a dwarf man and a hunchback woman) are depicted in poor light, as the hero and the heroine in the following *peruntiṇai* poem. A sexually charged dwarf approaches a hunchback woman with excessive passion. While engaging himself in a disgraceful dialogue with his ladylove, the dwarf overtly plays his personality and discreetly mocks her physical appearance to the amusement of readers. Here is the poem:[30]

Hunchback woman,
the way you move is gentle
and crooked as a reflection
in the water,
                    what good deeds
did you do that I should want you so?

        O mother! (she swore to herself) Some
        auspicious moment made you dwarf,
        so tiny you're almost invisible,
        you whelp born to a man-faced owl,
        how dare you stop us to say
        you want us? Would such midgets
        ever get to touch such as us!

Lovely one,
            curvaceous,
                        convex
as the blade of a plough,
you strike me with a love
I cannot bear.
            I can live
only by your grace.

        (Look at this creature!)
        You dwarf, standing piece of timber,
        you've yet to learn the right approach
        to girls. At high noon
        you come to hold
        our hand and ask us to your place.
        Have you had any women?

Good woman,
            Your waist is higher
than your head, your face a stork,
plucked and skinned,
with a dagger for a beak,
                        listen to me.
If I take you in the front, your hump
juts into my chest; if from the back
it'll tickle me in odd places.
                    So I'll not
even try it. But come close anyway and let's touch
side to side.

Chi, you're wicked. Get lost! You half-man!
As creepers hang on only to the crook of a tree
there are men who'd love to hold this hunch
of a body close, though nothing fits. Yet, you lecher,
you ask for us sideways. What's so wrong
with us?, you ball, you bush of a man.
Is a gentle hunchback type far worse than a cake
of black beans?

But I've fallen for you
(he said, and went after her).
O look, my heart,
at the dallying of this hunchback!

Man, you stand
like a creepy turtle stood up by somebody,
hands flailing in your armpits.
We've told you we're not for you. Yet you hang around.
Look, he walks now like *Kāma*.

Yes, the love-god with arrows, brother to *Cāma*.
Look at this love-god!
                    Come now, let's find joy,
you in me, me in you; come, let's ask and tell
which parts we touch.

I swear by the feet of my king.

All right, O gentle-breasted one. I too will give up
mockery.
                    But I don't want this crowd in the palace
laughing at us, screaming when we do it,
"Hey, hey! Look at them mounting,
leaping like demon on demon!"
                    O shape
of unbeaten gold, let's get away from the palace
to the wild jasmine bush. Come,
let's touch close, hug hard,
and finish the unfinished:
then we'll be
like a gob of wax on a parchment
made out in a court full of wise men,

and stamped
to a seal.
      Let's go.

(Marudaṉiḻa Nāgaṉār, *Kalittogai* 94,
tr. Ramanujan 1985:209–211)

"Note the unheroic, even antiheroic, mock-heroic quality of this unlovely couple, looking not for love but frankly for sex; the earthy humor … In a single phrase like "You whelp born to a man-faced owl," many categories are undone. The piece makes comedy and poetry by violating over and over the decorum of *akam* poems. The metaphors are bold, explicit. The two persons are not even young—one of them is "a stork, plucked and skinned." This is *peruntiṇai*, the "major type" depicting the common human condition, love among the misfits with no scruples regarding the niceties of time or landscape; moving from mockery to coupling in the course of a conversation. Their misfit is evident in their bodies' lack of fit. And they are obviously servants" (Ramanujan, *Op. cit.*, pp. 260–61), who throw away their decency to the wind while enacting their part. Being marginalised people, living in deplorable conditions, their depressed sexual feelings throw away the gentle words in the beginning and do away the decency at the end. "While the five middle *akam* categories have the most tightly structured symbolic language, the *peruntiṇai* is free and realistic, with real toads in real cesspools" (*Ibid.*, p. 261).

It is observed that the people of the depressed class would naturally tend to violate the social norms determined by the high caste or higher class. While questioning the values and customs dictated by the dominant class, they deliberately chose to uphold their age-old culture and tradition by terming them as 'genuine' and 'realistic.' Being deprived socially, economically and sexually and hence vigorously ruled by "ID," the behaviour psychology of the service class and the physically challenged seem to be 'unnatural' or 'obnoxious' in the eyes of others. If a person is "mind/heart/soul centric" (where the sensuous body is controlled by the strong mind), he/she behaves as a "normal human being" or "noble one" by adhering to the social norms and values. But if a person is "body-centric" (where the weak mind obliges the sensuous body), then obviously he/she behaves as an "abnormal entity" or "a demon"/"demoness" by not adhering to the social norms and values. The former is a 'genuine human being' (who is ruled by *man* > *manusya* [Skt.] *manam* > *manidan* [Tamil]) who is truly concerned for others' sentiment and wishes to lead a dignified life. Contrary to this, the latter is a 'fake human being' (*amānusya* [Skt.], *arakkan* (demon), [Tamil]) who does not care for others' sentiments or modesty. So, the dwarf man behaves as a rustic, extrovert, uncultured one, even while enacting the climax of the sexual act. He doesn't have a sense of guilt about his senseless words and absurd behaviour. Only he wants 'to finish the unfinished act' a little away from the eyes of the public just to get rid of their condemnation. Here lies the reality of physiology and psychology. The "basic instinct" (sexual feeling) is no doubt, a quite normal and genuine emotion to all human beings irrespective of their physical fitness or otherwise. Obviously, the mind plays a crucial role in anyone's sensual feelings and subsequently drives him/her to experience the pleasure of sexual acts in his/her own way. Pertinently, one should not assume that the physically challenged are devoid of the "desired sensation." When they get an opportunity to express their sexual passion, they would behave more adventurously and explicitly than the "perfect ones"/ "cultured ones," as they have no qualms about such things.

Contradicting some of the notions outlined in *kaikkiḷai* and *peruntiṇai* that the 'atypical love feelings' fit only the servants or workmen (*TKM.*, Akattiṇai Iyal 25–26), here is a poem from *Kalittogai*[31] depicting an old brahmin behaving uncharacteristically with a young woman who is waiting for her lover at night.

Taken aback by the dismal behaviour of the old man, she is narrating the incident to her *tōḻi*, after a tryst with him at night which turns out to be a fiasco.

My well-dressed friend,
listen to what happened.
It has set the whole village laughing.

It's the dead of night, very dark,
no sign of life,
and I'm waiting
all dressed up, lovely shawl,
best jewels,
for our soft broad-chested man,

when that old cripple, that brahman
turns up,
the one you're always asking me to respect,
bald head, rough blanket,
hands and legs shortened by leprosy,
the fellow who never leaves our street.

He bends low
to take a good look at me
and says,
   "Standing here
at this unearthly hour?
Who are you?"

He won't leave my side
like an old bull
who has sighted hay;
he opens his satchel, saying,
"Lady, come, have some betel, won't you?"

I stand there, say nothing.
"Listen, girl," he says,
   stepping back a little.
"I have caught you.
I'm a demon too, but not your kind.
Be good to me. If you trouble me,
I'll grab all the offerings of this village,

> And you'll get nothing."
> And he jabbers on.
> I can see by now the old fellow is a bit scared,
> may be thinking I'm some demon woman,
> so I pick up a fistful of sand and throw it
> in his face, and he howls and howls.
>
> It was as if a trap laid by hunters
> for a tiger, a fearless, striped, cruel-eyed tiger,
> had caught instead a puny jackal.
>
> What a sight for someone
> waiting to see a lover!
> The whole village is laughing
> at this old brahman whose life
> is a daily farce.
>
> (Kabilar, *Kalittogai* 65, tr. Ramanujan 1985:207–08)

The uncharacteristic, anti-statured and crazy behaviour of the elderly brahmin who also happens to be a priest of the local temple is observed here. Against the backdrop of Indian culture, wherein *purohit*s (priests), *brahmin*s (high caste men), *guru*s (mentors), *āchārya*s (teachers), parents, and elderly people are looked up to and greeted reverentially, this poem depicts the crude reality of the bygone Tamiḻ society. Though unfortunate, it is a fact that irrespective of time, place, creed, position, stature, class, profession, sex, age, etc., there exists in the history of mankind "the unscrupulous ones" i.e., "the sex fiends." The perverted mind prevails all the more in the realm of religion wherein 'black sheep' are brisk with their 'business' but implicitly, disguising themselves as the agents or the incarnations of Godhead.

Some interesting historical facts may be recalled here as the ancient Tamiḻ society which belongs to the 'Heroic Age' (*c*. 3000 BCE–300 CE) is evidently a secular one, wherein the king is everything. "Not rice, not water, only the king is the life-breath of a kingdom," thus says emphatically the poet Mōcikīraṉār (*PNU*

186). Contrary to the social structure based on *varṇāśrama dharma* (social hierarchical system based on birth/caste) preached and practised by the Aryans, the ancient Tamiḻ society has a social structure based on occupations. In the absence of temples, naturally, the priest class does not exist there. It is in the last phase of the 'Heroic Period,' gradually the Aryans/brahmins start entering the Tamiḻ territories leading to the emergence of countless shrines and priesthood classes. A majority of Tamiḻ literary works, spanning from the period of post-Sangam to modern period, reverentially speak of the brahmin to a great extent, yet a section of the aboriginals of Tamiḻ land united under the banner of 'Drāviḍar Kaḻagam' (The Federation of Dravidians), (1925) led by 'Periyār' E.V. Ramasamy (1879–1973), 'Pēraṟiñar' C.N. Annadurai (1909–1969) and others begin to express their critical views against the Aryans in their speech and works particularly after 1856 (the year of publication of the great research work entitled *A Comparative Grammar of the Dravidian or South Indian Languages* by Caldwell published by Harrison, London). But it is very strange rather unbelievable to hear a sort of anti-brahmin sentiment expressed in the aforesaid early Tamiḻ poem by Kabilar, a great poet of Sangam classics, who is of a brahmin lineage.

It is really intriguing to see that the old brahmin priest described in the poem is not only a cripple but also an ugly bloke with a bald head, rough blanket, and hands and legs shortened by leprosy. But he thinks of himself as a Romeo looking for beautiful women in the streets even in the dead of night. Expected to be a high person of respect at his dwelling place, the old priest behaves with a puerile attitude which is juxtaposed with his age, stature and position. He seems to have been a frustrated bachelor for a long time, driven out by ID exceedingly under duress, deliberately jabbering with the beautiful young girl only to satiate his sexual impulses. By the phrase of simile *ēdil kuṟunari* (lit. "a useless small fox" but translated as "a puny jackal" by A.K. Ramanujan), the poet Kabilar sarcastically paints the useless, cunning mind and crooked behaviour of the old priest to the amusement of the readers. The similes/metaphors like "an old bull who has sighted hay," and "a trap laid by hunters for a tiger had instead caught a puny jackal" are bold and explicit. The protagonists of the poem are not evenly depicted on any count, but they differ in age, beauty, and nature. The male psyche (though old enough) depicted in the poem does not bother at all about talking rubbish and stalking the unknown girl thereby sexually harassing her. Though extremely anguished over the ridiculous behaviour of 'the old, cracked nut,' she behaves with great poise and intelligence. The assertive woman, awaiting her lover who would any way protect her like a ferocious tiger, saves herself, her modesty, and her femininity all by her sheer presence of mind and justifiable behaviour. The woman's psyche ruled by "the sense of ego" here just looks for "homemaking" by meeting her lover in the dead of night, though clandestinely. Contrary to this positive behaviour, the old brahmin's psyche is depicted with negative attributes as he is over-driven by sexual impulses and drives. Hence, the significance of the following Tamil sayings: *kāmam kaṇṇai maṟaikkum* ("Lust blinds eyes"), *kāmattiṟkuk kaṇṇillai* ("Lust has no eyes").

Behavioural Psychology in *Kuṟiñci* Poems

Kuṟiñci, representing the mountain region, describes "the sexual union of lovers at midnight" and occupies the very first and prominent place among the "middle five love categories" of *akam* poetry. It is the only phase of the love category that wholly signifies *kaḷavu* (clandestine love). The term *kuṟiñci* denotes the famous flower *Strobilanthes Kunthianus* of the mountain region. The *Strobilanthes* (a shrub whose brilliant white or blue flowers blossom for only a few days once every twelve years) is symbolic in indicating the blossom of the feminine sense ready to get united with the male physically and spiritually. It is the 'basement' on which heroes and heroines build their mansion. The other four love themes (*mullai*, *marudam*, *neydal* and *pālai*) are actually 'apartments' of *kuṟiñci* since they are, in one way or other, referring to some aspect of "separation" (patient waiting, a husband visiting 'other woman' after marriage, anxious waiting and departing through the wilderness) that takes place after the union of lovers.

In the pre-marital love scenario, the hero and the heroine meet secretly—primarily aiming at "family making"—but only after overcoming several kinds of challenges and hazards. Having duly aroused themselves with sensual feelings, they shall have a blissful union when these adults meet in private in the dead of night. The behavioural psychology of men usually has the tendency of postponing the marriage, as long as possible, with their sweethearts in their self-interest. In doing so, they experience a unique sexual pleasure at the cost of their counterparts.

A hero of the mountain region in the anthology of *Akanā-nūṟu* (herein after *ANU*) develops a habit of meeting his ladylove at night and maintains the practice for a long period. He visits her regularly going through a dangerous path. *Tōḻi*, the confidante of the heroine, is worried about his safety as well as the pending marriage of her friend. So, she explicitly advises the hero who comes at night to visit them during the day at their orchard where honeycombs thrive. But she suggests to him implicitly to get married to her friend at the earliest. Let us look at the suggestion implicitly mentioned in the following poem.[32]

> Abundant spent flowers drop down, changing
> the color of the fierce forest stream, in which
> crocodiles lie, that rushes with swirls and
> crashes on tall rocks. The rapid flood waters
> drag a lonely, roaming elephant in rut.

Oh lord of the tall mountains! You are bold
and unafraid like a fierce boar, and you cross
the difficult shore at night. If something bad
happens to you one day my friend will not live
the next day. Even those who come regularly
on that path, which does not have hindrances,
could suffer sometimes. We will be distressed
and worried thinking about your night visits.

If you come during the day, you can unite with
my friend with curved, delicate arms that are
like bamboo pieces between nodes, protected
by our mother, in the vast mountain range,
in our fruit-filled orchard near the huge mountain
with honeycombs and soaring peaks,
under dense trees near beautiful *kānthal* bushes.

(Kabilar, *Akanāṉūṟu* 18, tr. Vaidehi Herbert)[33]

In the poem, the *tōḻi* makes it very clear to the hero that he should
stop coming during the night as her friend is really worried about
his safety. She points out the reasons—the fierce wild stream with
hiding crocodiles, gushing swirls, roaming of an elephant in rut
on the riverbed—and makes him understand their anxiety over his
adventure. She directly points out that if something bad happened
to him on the way then the next very moment her friend would
not live. Though she requests him to come during the day to unite
with her friend in their fruit-filled orchard near the curved mountain with honeycombs but subtly suggests that also might not
really be possible for him as tribal people would roam around the
region to collect honey from honeycombs. So, she obliquely suggests to him to wed her friend at the earliest as she is sincerely
concerned about the consummation of her friend's marriage. Here
we can understand how the woman's mind, especially in clandestine love, gets perturbed over the safety of her man as the latter is
truly worthwhile than her own life. When something dreadful
happens to the lover, it means that everything ceases to be for the

beloved who is yet to wed. Instantly like a pack of cards, her modesty, virtuous life, dream of family making, etc., all would crash down at the loss of her lover's life. Thus, realizing the danger involved with the life of secret love, the *tōḻi*, who is of assertive nature and has no self-interest, sincerely makes the hero understand her concern for the benefit of her friend and the latter, who just continues to experience the thrilling as well as the delightful part of life.

The same sort of message has been seen imparted in several of the ancient Tamiḻ poems, over and again, sometimes more strikingly through the same kind of assertive character viz. *tōḻi*. The ancient Tamiḻ mind, while dealing with delicate love feelings, largely depicts the heroes and the heroines exchanging their emotional feelings only through *tōḻi*. She is the daughter of foster-mother who happens to be the friend of the biological mother of the heroine. As she is sensible, realistic, genuine and thoughtful, always she conducts herself in the interest of her friend. She speaks on behalf of the latter as her conscience. She knows what is good for both the hero and the heroine. And so, she suggests, advises, encourages, soothes, and at times even admonishes them while fixing their flaws for betterment. In the following poem of *Kalittogai* anthology,[34] the *tōḻi* comes to know about the intended departure of the hero to an alien country in search of wealth. Finding fault with his unjustifiable behaviour, she puts forth the picture-perfect behaviours of worthy men for his consideration and due change of his mind.

> O lord of the shores where *thillai* trees
> and *mundakam* plants with dark flowers grow
> together on tall sand dunes decorating the
> seashore grove, and residing birds appear like
> blossoms of crooked *thāzhai* trees
> whose hanging fruits are like water-filled pots
> brought by the great Sivan to the trunk of
> a banyan tree! Listen!

> Guidance is to help those who are suffering.
> Caring is not to part from those united.
> Courtesy is knowing norms and behaving well.
> Kindness is not ruining relatives.
> Wisdom is tolerating the words of the ignorant.
> Kinship is not forgetting what one said.
> Steadfast is to be confidential not letting others know.
> Justice is to seize the lives of the wrong, no matter
> who they are.
> Patience is to tolerate those who do not care.
>
> If you understand these, lord, hitch the horses to
> your chariot and come to remove the distress of my
> friend with a beautiful forehead.
> To abandon her after enjoying her beauty is like
> discarding a pot after drinking its sweet milk!

(Nallanduvaṉār, *Kalittogai* 133, tr. Vaidehi Herbert)[35]

Thus, she emphatically conveys to the hero to take care of his beloved at any cost by not leaving her in solitude and suffering. So, she addresses him on noble conduct in the following words: "Goodness is helping others in distress; support is not deserting the dependent; culture is abiding by the conduct of the world; love is not severing the bonds with relatives; wisdom is disregarding the advice of the ignorant; honesty is not refuting his own words; integrity is ignoring others' mistakes; justice is seizing the lives of wrong without prejudice; patience is tolerating others who condemn." In these words of upright thought, we could see the functioning of the noble mind or behaviour psychology of the *tōḻi* who just wishes to win the heart of the hero by her alluring politeness and charming words of wisdom in the interest of her friend. Contextually, the behaviour psychology of the woman in the poem, as stated elsewhere, aims at "making home" whereas the behaviour of the man is not the same. The hero wishes to go abroad in search of wealth as his priority is now economic prosperity. He does not weigh his beloved's pitiable condition who is yet to marry him. He is not even sure when he will return to his place; however, he wishes to proceed. We could speculate on the psychological confrontation that exists here between the heroine and the hero. When the heroine is emotionally charged over him and concerned very much for her modesty, the hero is more concerned about material gain and unconcerned about her pathetic situation. So, we could see the prevailing mental tension or psychological clash between the couple with the following terms of binary opposition "heart" *vs.* "body" or rather "soul" *vs.* "physique." As the girlfriend of the heroine, she is worried about the physical and mental well-being of the latter, thus she conveys her concern adeptly with suitable words to see the couple wedded and lead family life peacefully in their own place.

Behavioural Psychology in *Mullai* Poems

Mullai, representing the forest region, depicts the patient waiting for ladylove on the outskirts in the evening for her husband who goes away in search of wealth or in the quest of carrying out royal duty or in the interest of gaining knowledge. The term *mullai* refers to the name of the specific flower of the forest region 'jasmine' (*Jasminum Auriculatum*). The flower growing abundantly in forest cum pastureland symbolically represents the married woman. Its white colour and exceptional fragrance respectively signify the 'pure' and 'blissful' life of married women. So, the behaviour psychology of the woman in *mullai* poems always pertains to her patient waiting at home and more so in taking care of her family in the absence of her husband. Contrary to the behaviour of women, men always go out in the quest of gaining wealth/wages/knowledge obviously for economic prosperity to manage their household and return after the completion of their mission. Here the dichotomy found between the couple's behaviour can be simply said as "homemaking" *vs*. "house management".

No heroine in the Sangam poetry, for any reason, ever wishes her lover/husband to leave her and go to an alien country. Being emotionally attached to their spouses, the wives in *mullai* just wish that they alone should offer sexual pleasure or sulking wholly to their respective husbands. They do not accept any excuse or tolerate any hindrance to play havoc in their relationship with their life partners—no matter whether it is weather or 'other woman'—obviously, they undergo severe mental tension as well as physical apprehension. Evidently, women never enjoy life in solitude. They would like to have their husbands at their place for physical pleasure as well as for soul peace. So does—a heroine tremble in *Narriṇai* (herein after *NRI*) anthology. Unable to face the monsoon season in the absence of her husband, she shares her agony with her friend. The poem follows:[36]

> May you live long, my friend!
> The land might turn upside
> down, but my lover does not
> swerve from his words.
>
> The clouds absorbed water
> from the full ocean, clustered
> together, grew dark and came
> down here as heavy rain with
> loud thunder strikes.
> I, without his graces,
> am in distress now like a broken
> tree branch that is burned at night
> by the cattle herders
> of the woodland. I am pitiable!
>
> (Maruṅgūrp Paṭṭiṉattuc Cēndaṉ Kumaraṉār,
> *Narriṇai* 289, tr. Vaidehi Herbert)[37]

The poem, narrated through the mouth of the heroine, just realistically portrays the actual dismal condition of young women whose husbands are away on some mission. The heroine is much worried over the arrival of monsoon season. Because her husband had assured her earlier that he would return by the arrival of the season. But he is yet to return. The little delay on his part distresses the heroine to a greater extent. The phrase of simile in the poem "a broken tree that is burned at night by cattle herders" just illustrates so explicitly the heroine's anxiety and depression in every aspect. While the noun phrase "a broken tree" just indicates her pathetic condition, the possible gossip of her neighbours is suggestively rendered with the phrase "tree that is burned at night by cattle herders of the woodland." Despite her unfortunate situation, the heroine still firmly bets on her lover's conduct and commitment. Hence, she expresses her sense of hope in the very beginning of her dialogue itself with her friend, "the land might move away but my lover does not swerve from his words." Thus, we can comprehend here the conflicting psychological behaviour of the heroine in which both the realistic and optimistic senses are simply essayed more beautifully.

While this is a behaviour pattern of *mullai* heroines, the heroes have certain behaviours according to the needs of situations. It is not so with the heroes as they willingly depart from their beloveds. Almost all the heroes feel sick of leaving their sweethearts at home. Several of them even admonish their mind (while still in the middle of the mission in a barren land) pushing them to undertake a journey through the wilderness for the sake of material benefits (Paraṇar, *KRT* 120). Some heroes in the middle of the journey even become emotionally sick over their lady-loves and chide their minds/hearts too. Remembering his beloved's beautiful physical features, a hero in the following poem (*KRT* 131) expresses his hopeless situation:[38]

> Her arms have the beauty
> of a gently moving bamboo
> Her large eyes are full of peace.

> She is faraway,
> her place not easy to reach.
> My heart is frantic
> with haste,
>> a plowman with a single plow
>> of land all wet
>> and ready for seed.

(Ōrēruḻavaṉār, *Kuṟuntogai* 131,
tr. Ramanujan 1985:75)

Here in the poem, the visibly forsaken hero by the urge of sexual feelings duly remembers his wife's extraordinary, beautiful arms and eyes. Having understood the vitality of "basic instincts" now he finds fault with his mind which prompts him to depart from his wife. Being deprived of the blissful physical relationship with his wife, he craves it though he is placed far away. The words in the phrase, "a plowman with a single plow, of land all wet and ready for seed," all indeed implicitly suggest that everything is related to the act of sexual union. While he is "a plowman" that he himself refers to "a single plow" signifies "his genitals," "land all wet" strikingly refers to "his passionate wife," and the last phrase "ready for seed" just implies "his physical and mental preparedness to have union with his wife." By this sort of sketch depicting the heroes as longing for physical encounters, of course with their wives, one can consider the notion that "men are mightier only in physique but weaker in mind." This is what again is perfectly depicted in the following poem too.[39] A husband just after returning home from afar, unusually yet poetically eulogies his beloved's gait, her forehead, and her glance:

> Because peacocks moved like you
> and jasmine opened
> like your brow
> and does had scared looks like you

> my girl,
> thinking of you, your lovely brow,
> I've come
> faster than the rains.

(Pēyanār, *Aiṅkuṟunūṟu* 492, tr. Ramanujan 1985:78)

As the hero has just returned home after a long period of separation, naturally he is deprived of physical as well as emotional bonding with his wife. So, driven by impulse, he at once becomes a brilliant poet. Whether conscious or otherwise, he pleases his beloved, making her feel shy. One could see the 'signifiers' and 'signified' employed unusually here in the similes of the poem. This is typical of the behavioural psychology of men—returning home after a long period of separation—who go out on some mission or other. In such contexts, men characteristically try to please their wives with the utmost nice words, and shower generous gifts but with self-interest i.e., "the physical gratification."

It is true that a man—who was away from his wife for a long period—would always speed up his vehicle to reach his beloved's place as early as possible. But the behaviour of some heroes as depicted in Sangam classics is strangely quite pleasing and really courteous. In a *mullai* poem,[40] a hero emotionally charged over his wife is returning through a forest/pastureland tract. Though he is very eager to reach home at the earliest to make himself and his beloved wife happy, yet on his way back he advises his charioteer to slow down the chariot. It sounds quite unrealistic but one could see how the ancient Tamil mind works even under the duress of physical impulses and drives.

> Rains in season,
> forests grow beautiful.
> Black pregnant clouds
> bring flower and blue-gem
> flower on the bilberry tree
> the red-backed moths multiply,

and fallen jasmines
cover the ground.
                    It looks like
a skilled man's work of art,
this jasmine country.

Friend, drive softly here.
Put aside the whip for now.
Slow down
these leaping pairs of legs,
these majestic horses
galloping in style
as if to music.

Think of the stag, his twisted antlers
        like banana stems
        after the clustering bud
        and the one big blossom
        have dropped,

think of the lovely bamboo-legged doe
ready in desire:

if they hear the clatter
of horse and chariot,
how can they mate
at their usual dead of night?

(Cīttalai Cāttaṉār, *Akanāṉūṟu* 134,
  tr. Ramanujan 1985:76–77)

Here in the poem, the courteous words of a kindhearted hero (the signifier) who wishes to control his charged mind (signified as galloping horses), come out through his presence of mind and thoughtful behaviour. Though his mind is emotionally charged with sexual "impulses and drives" (ID), yet he attempts to reach the status of "Super Ego" by instructing the charioteer to slow down the speed of galloping horses—so that the pairs of stag and doe—assume to be ready in desire—shall not be disturbed. Here one could see the "superhuman mind" and his "superior conduct" aesthetically essayed in the poem though stretched a little.

Behavioural Psychology in *Marudam* Poems

Marudam, representing the agricultural pastureland tract, portrays verbal as well as mental conflicts that take place between wife and husband (due to the unfaithfulness of the latter) at early morning hours before sunrise. The term *marudam* is named after the Terminalia Arjuna tree (*Lagerstroemia Speciosa*). The location is fertile, watery countryside. The hero of cropland tract enjoying life in blooming condition with abundant resources often maintains extramarital relationship with young and beautiful women. The behavioural psychology of *marudam* men is related to maintaining of extramarital relationship with unmarried women. **No married woman in Sangam poems is depicted as having illicit relationship with anyone other than her lover**. Though she sulks over the unfaithfulness of her husband, never does she abandon him. She takes care of her family and children with added responsibility. Obviously, the behavioural psychology of the virtuous wife and the unfaithful husband can be seen in binary terms as "body-centric" *vs.* "soul-centric" or "home making" *vs.* "home breaking."

Not all but only a few men, who are ruled by sexual impulses and drives, strong in body but weak in mind, tend to keep other women for sensual pleasure. They do not really seem to be worried about their immoral activity and its ill consequences. Pained over the infidelity of the man, it is only the wife more than anybody else who suffers mentally and physically, inwardly and outwardly, inside the home in private and in public. Though shattered over the unfaithfulness of her husband, the wife sustains the pressure just in the interest of her children and family. More often, some wives who are unable to overcome the distress and setback because of their men's fault, commit suicide and their children become orphaned. It is heartening to know that these sorts of serious consequences are not depicted in the Sangam classics while they deal with the unfortunate love theme i.e., "unfaithfulness of men."

Often in the *marudam* love poems, the hopeless situation of the heroines, unfaithfulness of men and the physical beauty of concubines are described through the features and behaviours of birds and animals. In the poems of Sangam classics, **no wife or her *tōḻi* ever accuses the unfaithful hero directly blaming his immoral behaviour.** The wives/*tōḻi*s always demonstrate their unhappiness, sulking and anger in subtle words just in the hope that their men would correct their unbecoming behaviour sooner or later. Their discreet, gentle and modest "adoptive behaviour" usually acts as the catalyst in bringing their men to senses and thereby saving their family. The following poem[41] shows how a heroine acts with a sense of decorum/decency at the hour of crisis. She comes to know that her husband has decided to marry a mistress of his liking. Consequent upon it, she becomes anxious but tries to save her family, the ship which is drowning swiftly. So, she expresses her feelings thus:

> O man from the town, where
> hating to stand in the mud,
> a red-eyed buffalo tied to
> a strong rope broke loose,
> lifted a sharp thorn fence,
> jumped into a pond with
> stagnant water, caused fish
> to dart away and *vaḷḷai* vines
> with beautiful hollow stems
> to get tangled,
> and ate the watery lotus flowers
> on which bees were swarming!

Who are you to us to quarrel?
They say that you brought someone
with dark, hanging hair like flowing
water into our house and married her.
We did not say that.
May you live, long my lord!
If my bangles that are bright like Aḷḷūr,
rich in paddy, owned by victorious king
Cheḻiyaṉ who won difficult battles against
enemies with elephants and crushed them
with his bright swords, slip, let them slip.

Lord! You can go where you want to go!
Who is there to stop you?

(Aḷḷūr Naṉmullaiyār, *Akanāṉūṟu* 46,
  tr. Vaidehi Herbert)[42]

The heroine just implicitly scorns the infidelity of her husband
who is unfaithful to her for some time. Here she employs the term
"robust buffalo" ('the hero,' the "signified") and minutely sket-
ches the act of satiating its appetite i.e., eating watery 'lotus
flower' ('harlot,' the "signified") secretly at night. She skilfully
refers to the unfaithful behaviour of her husband who pays his
secret visit to her place and enjoys his mistress at the unearthly
hour. Furthermore, while referring to her husband's daring act of
bringing his concubine for sexual enjoyment, she shrewdly puts
the words as the gossip of others. She says: "They say that you
brought someone with dark, hanging hair into our house and
started enjoying her." Thereafter, she shrewdly tries to gain his
sympathy by greeting him as: "May you live long my lord" and
by putting forth her pitiable condition in the next phrase as: "My
bangles that are bright … slip, let them slip. Lord! You can go
where you want to go! Who is there to stop you?" Without upset-
ting the apple cart of his sensual mood and questioning his immoral activity, the heroine tactfully handles the worst crisis of her
life by approaching her husband as a servant does to the master.
All these efforts are just to get her husband back. So, the confron-

tation/clash/conflict between herself and her husband can be viewed in terms of binaries like "Ego" *vs.* "ID"; "heart/soul" *vs.* "body/physique"; "home making" *vs.* "home breaking"; "inner world" *vs.* "outer world."

While the heroine in *akam* poetry becomes unhappy over the unfaithfulness of her husband, she consciously never quarrels neither with him nor with his concubine. She handles the grim situation very tactfully; hides her "aggrieved mind"/"pained heart." Approaching the hero as if she concedes him, she puts the blame on her aged body and on her son at times. At several instances, she implicitly slights the hero and his paramour only to conquer them by her gentle behaviour. This is how she saves her family, the slow drowning ship. She embarrasses him by saying, "Yesterday, you played, embracing your lover. Today you came here and told me that I have budding breasts with pallor on my lovely chest. I am a woman with faultless chastity, and I am your son's mother. You are using confusing words that lie. You are teasing my maturity. That fits me fine. My youth … has left me a long ago. How can your lies be sweet to me?" (Paraṇar, *ANU* 6).

In another *marudam* poem, while the heroine sees her husband's concubine approach her son who is playing in the street with affection, she does win her by charming words. She narrates the incident to her husband as and how she handled the embarrassing situation: "I saw her (concubine) standing there. I did not go away. O faultless woman! Why are you embarrassed? You are his mother too. I said quickly embracing her. She stood ashamed, and looked down as if she were a thief, and scratched the ground with her toe. Lord, how could not I love her? She was a like a precious goddess from the skies, who is like a mother to your son" (Cāgālacaṉār, *ANU* 16). She speaks and behaves so delightfully only to win her "home breakers" at any cost. By praising the concubine's beauty as well as treating her as another mother for her son, she makes her feel utterly ashamed. By conveying her graceful remarks on her, she makes her husband also feel ashamed and mend his ways. Her behavioural psychology does wonders in this delicate private matter. Another heroine behaves differently and tells her unfaithful husband, "You are so desirable to your women, but I am one with love for my son" (Pāṇḍiyaṉ Kāṉappēreyil Tanda Uggira Peruvaḻudi, *ANU* 16). Thereby she drives her husband to become emotional about his son. Soon he says that he too has love for their son. Following this he hugs her and becomes her own man at the end.

Behavioural Psychology of Concubines in *Marudam* Poems

In several *marudam* poems, the concubine sometimes boldly walks into the street of her paramour to show her beauty just to tease and make his wife upset. The hardnosed mistress speaks to her friend in the following poems: "They say that the wife of the man from the town with bright shores links us with her husband and fights, even if we are not doing anything, since she is unable to live with it. Let's go there and walk, letting our stacked bangles jingle, my friend! Let her beat her stomach!" (Ālaṅkuḍi Vaṅkaṉār, *ANU* 106). Limiting her antagonism only to her man a mistress says, "They say that his wife is angry with me. He does not have rights to my stacked bangles ... We are not enemies to his wife! Her husband, who abandons women turning their beautiful brows pale, is the enemy with whom she is living" (Paraṇar, *ANU* 186). Evidently, she avoids blaming the heroine directly but does openly blame her fancy man. While blaming her fancy man, a mistress in a poem implicitly shows her respect to his wife: "He talks big in my place. But when he is at his home, he is like a dancing puppet that lifts its hands and legs again and again reflecting the wishes of his son's mother" (Ālaṅkuḍi Vaṅkaṉār, *KRT* 8). **Evidently in *marudam* poems, the unfaithful husbands virtually come back to their wives at the end.** Their son becomes a binding factor for the couple's reunion. This is a realistic working factor in India which indeed takes care of families from possible wreckages for ages.

Vāyil Maṟuttal (Door Shutting): Behavioural Psychology of angry Heroines

In the convention of *akam* poetry, bards occasionally act as messengers between sulking wives and unfaithful husbands to pacify the anger of the former. Being frustrated over the faltering attitude of their men, sometimes the wives take the extraordinary step of "door shutting" (*vāyil maṟuttal*, literally enacted at the door which is shut in the face of the unfaithful husband returning from his mistress's place early in the morning) to express their aversion/hatred over the illicit relationship of their counterparts. Though the affected wives get agitated to some extent, they behave with poise. Again, their conduct of "door shutting" is not for rejecting their husbands permanently but just for conveying their unhappiness thereby making their counterparts realize the mistake at least for some time. A hero along with a bard approaches his estranged wife for mending the ties. But the wife refuses entry for his dillydallying attitude and promptly sends them back. The following poems deal plainly with this aspect.[43]

> Oh man from a town
> where a housewife gives large
> quantities of harvested lentils
> to the bard's daughter with sharp
> teeth, in exchange for *keḻiru* fish
> that she brings in her large bowl!
>
> My friends wearing fine jewels
> and I are aware that you utter many
> lies, just like your bard.
>
> (Ōrampōgiyār, *Aiṅkuṟunūṟu* 47,
>   tr. Vaidehi Herbert)[44]

Oh man from a town where a wife
pours year-old white paddy
into a basket emptied of *varāl* fish
brought by the naive, white-toothed
daughter of a bard, handy with nets!
I do not desire for you to come here,
oh lord, bearing marks made by your
mistress!

(Ōrampōgiyār, *Aiṅkuṟunūṟu* 48,
  tr. Vaidehi Herbert)[45]

The courteous behaviour as well as the firmness of the heroine who does not wish to allow the hero and his bard for the former's shillyshallying mind and non-mending attitude is portrayed here. As usual, the hero returns from his mistress's house after spending the whole night with her. But this time, he returns to her bearing the marks made by his concubine on his body. Thereupon, the wife becomes intolerant. Moreover, he has not changed his attitude even after many days of sulking. Angry and upset over his improper behaviour, she is determined to teach him a lesson at the end so that he might mend his ways. For all the mess up in her life, she finds fault with the bard whom she considers as a pimp. Even then, she does not wish to blame her man strongly but with little concern. So, she says, "You are a liar just like your bard." The poems strikingly underline the culture/behaviour of "home makers" (wives) while condemning the hero and his bard. Again, in these poems too, the hero who is ruled by sexual impulses and drives (ID) behaves typically as a "home breaker" while his counterpart is wholly concerned about "home making."

Behavioural Psychology in *Neydal* Poems

Neydal, representing the seashore region, depicts the anxious waiting of the heroine. She ponders over in the afternoon hours before sunset either in pre-marital or post-marital love situation due to the delayed return of her lover/husband at the stipulated time. The term *neydal* is named after the flower 'water lily' (*Nymphae Stellate*). *Neydal* poems largely describe the pangs of separation of the beloveds/wives against the background of sea-shore, wherein their personal affair becomes a fodder for gossip.

The heroes who go away to an alien country—before or after marriage, either for gaining wealth, defending his land, or acquiring knowledge—sometimes fail to return to their places at the appropriate time for genuine reasons. **No hero is ever depicted in *neydal* poems as enjoying the time while being away from their sweethearts**. Obviously, they remember their ladyloves with fond memories and, of course, with crestfallen heart. The heroes—especially those who are away in foreign lands to gain wealth—often think of their beloveds during their mission. Thereupon, they bemoan their fate, struggling all alone away from their darlings. Here are the poems of the lovers/husbands who speak to their hearts, realistically portraying their depressed minds:[46]

My heart! Your desire to get her
who is far away and hard to get,
is like a stork with ruined feathers
living near the waves of the eastern
ocean trying to catch fish that is hard to
get from the shores of Poṟaiyaṉ's Toṇḍi.

Fate is the reason for your sadness.

(Paraṇar, *Kuṟuntogai* 128, tr. Vaidehi Herbert)[47]

In summer she is cool like the
wood of sandal trees that grow
on the harsh Pothiyil mountain
range, where fierce gods reside
unknown to stable lives on earth.

> In winter she is warm, like the
> heart of the lotus flowers that collect
> and keep within the beautifully
> moving warmth of the sun and
> close when the rays of the sun
> leave.
>
> (Paḍumarattu Mōcikoṟṟaṇār, *Kuṟuntogai* 376,
>   tr. Vaidehi Herbert)[48]

Here in these poems, the heroes—after suffering physically and mentally in an alien country, in scorching sun and biting cold—understand that their minds acted in haste that went behind wealth, leaving his beloved, who too suffer like them in loneliness. The normal human mind is here depicted in these poems. When some-one worthy or something valuable is easily accessible and is with us for a quite long time then we treat him/her or it/that as an ordinary entity. Their worth comes to haunt us when that one/that thing is out of our sight or out of our reach. A man craves all the more genuinely, if that entity happens to be his own conjugal partner. In such situations, naturally man's analytical mind sees the hard reality with the experience gained cum awareness. Ordinarily, men are hesitant, cautious and shy to admit their flaws and mistakes to anyone but not to their own mind. Their old fashioned "conscience or conscious mind" of the past, on becoming a new "analytical or super conscious mind" at present surely would admonish them for the pitiable state of situation. This is what we observe in the functions of the *neydal* heroes' "analytical mind cum behaviour psychology" which are the outcome of "personal experience along with the effect of afterthought." We could see the two-fold conflicting functions in the psyche of *neydal* heroes whose present "analytical minds" (fondly remembering their wives) indict their own "obsessed minds" (in search of wealth) of the past. In a way, it reflects the two clashing sentiments—one representing the "material world" (concerned for economic prosperity) and the other "emotive world" (craving for sensual pleasure).

While this is the dismal condition of heroes who suffer emotionally, that of the heroines' is more pathetic and worrisome as they wholly depend on their counterparts for everything. Especially, when a man thinks of going away for gaining wealth, his ladylove normally trusts him. In the event of an unfortunate situation when he decides to forsake her, she just shows her pitiable conditions. "If he leaves, the lord of the vast ocean shores ... what else do I have other than my sweet life to lose?" (Iḷambhūdaṉār, *KRT* 334), so plainly expresses a heroine about her pathetic situation to her friend. While their husbands who departed earlier are delayed in their homecoming for on some reason or other the emotional mind of wives naturally experiences hardship on several counts. Particularly, in the days of pre-marital love, if the lover does not turn up at the stipulated period and behaves indifferently, then the beloved's mind/heart feels shattered and tormented. Let us observe the following poem:[49]

> My heart aches! My heart aches!
> Like the new flowers of the densely
> growing, tiny-leaved *nerunji* plants
> of the arid land, that appear sweet
> to the eyes but yield thorns later,
> my lover who used to be sweet has
> become cruel now. My heart aches!
>
> (Aḷḷūr Naṉmullaiyār, *Kuṟuntogai* 202,
>   tr. Vaidehi Herbert)[50]

Upon his delayed home coming, people doubting her modesty gossip inhumanly. It takes away her physiological and psychological strength. Besides the social stigma she faces, the unconcerned attitude (keeping her locked inside the home and watching her movements with eagle eyes) of her parents also makes her life really hell. As she becomes proverbially an orphan in the absence of her lover, she feels so depressed. Unable to withstand the winter season especially at midnight, she trembles emotionally too by saying: "It appears that I might not live" as scripted in the following poem.[51]

> It seems that my lover will not
> be back in this cold season that causes
> pain to those who are separated,
> when the north winds spray cold droplets,
> and a red-beaked stork shivers in pain
> and searches for prey on the cold, trembling
> mud piled up by fierce floods, its feathers
> like the flower petals of *murukkam* trees.
>
> It appears that I might not live, my friend!
>
> (Vāyilāṉ Dēvaṉār, *Kuṟuntogai* 103,
>   tr. Vaidehi Herbert)[52]

The poem thus realistically portrays the hopeless situation wherein the heroine undergoes mental depression as well as physical discomfort. Anxiety, the primordial mood of the *neydal* poetry is deep and pathetic since a woman has already gifted herself to a man. Unless he returns and marries her, she is virtually ruined. "The woman values and guards above all her "sexual honor" or "chastity" (*kaṟpu*) and her "virtue" and "modesty" (*nalaṉ*). As the man fears disgrace, cowardice, turning his back on the enemy, she constantly fears betrayal and abandonment by her man," (Ramanujan, *Op. cit.*, pp. 289–90). It needs to be mentioned here that **lovers in *neydal* poems abandon their beloveds only temporarily in the interest of gaining wealth for taking care of the household.** Again, in this love theme too, the prevailing cardinal point is "home making." The "adoptive behaviour" of the heroine which once allowed the hero to go out for obvious reasons, now changes its stand due to her own physical (possibly in the family way) and social pressures. So, she is obviously determined to lead the graceful family life like others by bearing children with the man to whom she had offered herself earlier. Again interestingly, **there is no poem in *neydal* too that depicts the hero or heroine as deserting his/her counterpart and marrying someone else.** Their behaviour is quite positive and truly intended for "home making" at the end, though they suffer physically and mentally in between for some time.

Behavioural Psychology in *Pālai* Poems

Pālai, representing the desert region/parched wasteland tract, portrays the feeling of separation. The theme "separation," as such, is so cardinal for all love themes except *kuṟiñci*, the lovers' union. The theme drives the lovers apart at noon of the scorching summer, either in pre-marital or post-marital love situation. The term *pālai* is named after the plant *Blue-dyeing Rosebay* or the tree *Wrightia* (*Wrightia Tinctoria*). The barren or wasteland is not seen as being a naturally occurring ecology. It is the region where the mountain (*kuṟiñci*) and the forest (*mullai*) meet each other and lose their natural characteristics during the peak summer days.

Behavioural Psychology of Foster-Mother

Two kinds of separation take place in the love theme of *pālai*. One is the hero going away alone leaving his beloved/wife in search of wealth or for joining the battle through wilderness on hot summer days. The other is the hero and the heroine together leaving (*uḍaṉpōkku*, the "elopement") their parents and all kith and kin and proceeding to an unknown place through wasteland on hot summer days only to start a family life against their wishes. Their movement is from *kuṟiñci* (mountain region) to *mullai* (forest, the pastoral region) then from *mullai* to *pālai* (the wasteland) i.e., "interior to exterior through another interior."

The first type of separation is the predominant one which describes the visible hazardous wasteland and the imperceptible mental distress of the heroine. *Tōḻi*, a dramatic persona, is the only soul mate who stands by her when the lover leaves her friend. *Uḍaṉpōkku* (elopement), the other type of separation, though not predominant yet realistically pictures the devastated feelings of mothers known as *narrāy* (*naṉ-mai+tāy*, i.e., One's own mother) and *cevilittāy* (foster-mother) another dramatic persona in *akam* poetry. *Cevilittāy* is the biological mother of the *tōḻi* who also happens to be the friend of the heroine's biological mother. She is the person, who actually takes care of the heroine since her birth till the day she goes away with a man to unknown place. Naturally, she has the emotional bonding with the heroine. Subsequently, the behavioural psychology of this persona is different from her daughter (*tōḻi*) as well as that of the biological mother of the heroine.

Her affection truly ponders over the safety and well-being of the heroine. Treating her foster-daughter still as an innocent girl, she wonders, "How did she become so strong to walk rapidly on the waterless harsh path, protected by her young man?" (Kayamaṉār, *KRT* 356). Blaming the young man responsible for all untoward incidents the foster-mother cries out, "She (the foster-daughter) did not think about me, the mother who gave birth to her and raised her. Our fine house with sky-high walls is lonely" (Ammūvaṉār, *ANU* 35); "With praises of the man from the mountain country, and awed by his lies, my daughter does not think about our huge house which is like a shady pond, or our wealth, and has gone with him on the wasteland paths" (Tāyaṅkaṇṇaṉār, *ANU* 105). Here the mother's psyche becomes too emotional and does not wish to see the reality of her daughter's adult world. Parents in India strongly feel that their wards do not have reasoning or analytical minds in the matter of selecting their life partners. Hence, the psyche of the foster-mother feels utterly sad: "I am not sorry for my daughter who went with a young man with the strength of a bull elephant. Separated from her, I am like the bellows blown in a furnace. My heart is sad, and I cannot sleep. I see her in my dreams (Māmūlaṉār, *ANU* 55). **The typical behaviour of foster-mother is always mentally worrying for the physical well-being of her foster-daughter.** She has nostalgia for her foster-daughter who enjoyed the comforts at home earlier and now struggling in the wilderness.

Though she is disgusted with the foster-daughter's elopement the *cevilittāy* wholeheartedly wishes as every mother does at the end. "May there be heavy shade without sun! May there be sand spread on the small mountain paths! May there be cool rains in the wasteland where she went, abandoning us, our innocent, dark girl who has gone with her young man bearing a bright, long spear!" (Kayamaṉār, *KṚT* 378); "If our great love for her will work, may the villages and old towns on her path be filled with people who take care of those who travel and own nothing" (Māmūlaṉār, *ANU* 15); "May he praise her with desire, embrace her fine beauty and hold her to his chest as she sleeps!" (Ammūvaṉār, *ANU* 35). But **the heroes who go away with their ladyloves never show any anti-feeling towards anyone including the biological and foster-mothers of their sweethearts** as they are happily accompanied by their beloveds.

The hero, who usually travels through wilderness, faces several kinds of hazards including the sudden attacks of reptiles/animals, of robbers/bandits and other hardships. Often, he goes away leaving his beloved/wife in search of gaining wealth which is essentially required for managing the household. For the same reason, he also undertakes the journey either to join the royal duty to protect his country or to acquire knowledge. "We should also remember that *pālai* is one phase of a cycle—he is going away from his woman "for education, work, earning wealth, war"—all *puṟam* concerns. Among the patterns between *akam* and *puṟam*, household and the world, one should include the rhythm of a man going out into the world and coming back into the family. Only a warrior who dies or an ascetic who renounces does not return— both are themes for *puṟam* poems. He passes through the *pālai* wilderness on his way to do "the world's work," and survives by remembering his home and women, in the heat and wildfire of the outer desert and the inner. Of course, heat and wildfire for the separated lover have sexual overtones" (Ramanujan, *Op. cit.*, p. 264).

Though the "separation cum journey" is a must and crucial one to a man—who has just become or is likely to become a family man sooner or later—yet normally no heroine or *tōḻi* happily accepts his decision. They try their level best to stop their men from proceeding further. When a situation demands then they oblige but of course not wholeheartedly. Their mind or psyche naturally tends to fear for the safe return of their beloveds for several reasons. The anxiety of heroines/*tōḻi*s is not because of any phobia but due to realistic, dangerous environmental situations wherein such travelers become the victims of the sudden attack by robbers/bandits, or any reptiles/animals. Let us see, how a heroine describes her mental agony to her friend in the poem following:[53]

> "He will not stay away for long,
> and yet you do not stop worrying,"
> you say, friend.
>
> In the hot, frightening wilderness he has entered,
> wild young warriors whose shouts echo on forking paths
> test their arrow shots,
> killing travelers, even though they have no money,
> and feed them to the birds.
> There, while foxes move around them,
> vultures eat fat,

>their strong, close-set claws bloody
>as they sit on a large-trunked *yā* tree,
>on a branch as thick as the trunk of the elephant
>that killed the northern newcomers,
>crushing their soft heads,
>when Iḷamperuñceṉṉi, the Chōḻa king,
>whose thick arms always gain victory in battle,
>sure in his shining fame,
>crushed the fortress of Pāḻi with its coppery walls
>to finish the work of his line.
>
>Even though I know he will return safely,
>my eyes, friend, refuse to stop crying.
>
>(Iḍaiyaṉ Cēndaṅkoṟṟaṉār, *Akanāṉūṟu* 375,
>   tr. Hart 1979:134)

Thus, the *pālai* heroine is typically worried over the safety and well-being of her beloved who has already set his foot in the wildest tract in search of wealth. Here in the poem, the wild young warriors (presumably thieves) behave characteristically as demons sucking the precious life of travellers just for nothing. As they are driven by the "impulses of basic needs" such as thirst and hunger, clothing and other materials, they do not mind acting ruthlessly worse than animals like wild vultures, foxes, and elephants. In spite of these hazards, the heroes knowingly undertake such journeys by putting their own lives at risk for the sake of "managing the household." As such they are not put off by "the impulses of satiating their selfish needs or desires" in the wilderness.

Though earning wealth is very essential for the obvious reason stated above, **the wives/*tōḻi*s do not wish their men going away**. In *Kalittogai,*[54] a hero, soon after his marriage, plans to go to an alien country to gain wealth. Unable to withstand even a short break cracking the emotional bonding of her husband and also not in a position to bear his physical absence, his wife does not wish him to take up the mission. She just shares her sensuous feeling and anxiety to her confidante. In turn, the heroine conveys rather convinces the hero to abandon the journey for obvious reasons.

> Lord, do not consider leaving, goaded by your
> mind, and thirsting for precious wealth!
> Think about the *thoyyil* designs that you painted
> on my arms lovingly, and the pallor spots I got
> embracing your mighty chest
> Wealth does not lie around for those who go in
> search of it. Also, those who do not leave to earn
> wealth do not starve.
>
> Will those with youth and love for each other
> desire to seek material wealth? Living life is living
> with love, embracing each other with one hand and
> covering torn clothes with the other hand.
> It is not possible to bring back youth that would be lost!
>
> (Pālai Pāḍiya Peruṅkaḍuṅkō, *Kalittogai* (*Pālaikkali*) 18,
>   tr. Vaidehi Herbert)[55]

One could see here, how differently the minds of newly married women and men perceive and function in a given context. Men cannot overstay at home, though just married, without earning money/wealth or material. In ancient times, everyone ought to put in their labour, their efforts with no layoff in order to manage their homes. Men who toil in land, serve in army, do any sort of business or go out in search of wealth are duly respected. So, the husband in the poem wishes to go out to earn money and thereby earn due respect and reputation. However, the newly married woman's mind perceives the hard reality from an emotional angle. The clash between the minds of man and woman here is thus "economic motives" *vs.* "emotive desires." We need to understand the woman's mind rightly here in the given context. The husband is the only person (the former lover who has become husband now) acquainted with the newly married woman at her new home. Nonetheless, for her the husband is everything, who takes care of her material needs as well as her physical/emotional desires. The *tōḻi* puts forth her pragmatic views to the hero saying: "Do not leave her (heroine) for the sake of wealth. Will those with youth and love go in search of it? Life means (for couple) living together with love and sharing everything that they have— may be a bit of torn cloth. Youth once lost is permanently lost. We can't bring back." The same message is emphatically imparted here but now, by a hero with a sarcastic tone as follows: "If the wealth that can be earned by going through the wasteland ... can give happiness, it does not give the splendour that youth can give. If youth once goes away, one cannot enjoy wealth that does not last forever. My heart! If wealth is what you desire, may your actions succeed!" (Unknown poet, *NRI* 126).

By these words, we can understand the pragmatic minds of the *tōḻi*, the girlfriend and of the poet (who assumes the role of the hero in the later poem), both representing the type of "assertive behaviour" as stated earlier. Virtually they both suggest to the men to abandon the intended journey. The behaviour of the *tōḻi* (presumably told by the heroine herself) and that of the poet here is very clear, realistic, and understandable. By spelling out justifiable reasons with no hesitation, they just maintain their typical "assertive behaviour," even while dealing with the so delicate a matter of the women. The newly married couple has not yet thoroughly enjoyed the blissful part of their conjugal life. The wife is yet to conceive. So, they cannot be said to make a family now unless they bear a child. As the friend and the poet (the hero presuming himself as a third person expressing his views to his own heart) are really concerned about the couple's blissful family life, they urge him to consider their words. The behavioural conduct of the heroes in the poems discussed above seems to be of "adoptive nature" as the literary personae maintain a stoic clam over their counsel. The conflicting behavioural pattern emerging out of the poems is "emotive concern" *vs.* "economic motives."

In one of the poems of *pālai* category, "the emotive mind" and "adoptive behaviour" of the heroine is well depicted. It is quite natural that after some days of marriage, the intimacy or emotional bonding of couples gradually would lessen. When there are some shortcomings in their expectations on any of the matters, then their apple cart cannot move further in the right direction. In the following poem, a man in need of wealth, who is also presumably unhappy over the beauty of his (supposedly) unfair lady, wants to go away from his wife to earn it. But his wife, who is over enthusiastic about his manliness, does not wish to miss him even for a moment. She shares her emotive feelings to her *tōḻi* without any inhibition. Thereby we come across a heroine of different behaviour. Consider the following poem.[56]

> Even if my lover does not shower
> his grace or love me, it is sweet to
> see him many times.
> My happiness is like that of a
> short-legged cripple who sits under
> a huge honeycomb, eyes it, cups his
> hands, points to it and then licks
> his empty palms with joy,
> in the tall mountain with swaying
> *koothali* vines.

> (Paraṇar, *Kuṟuntogai* 60, tr. Vaidehi Herbert)[57]

Evidently, the woman in this love poem places (presumably) her handsome husband on a high pedestal whereas herself at the bottom. Also, she does not feel shy to share her crush/passion over her majestic husband in the following words, "Just to see him is sweet to my mind." This sort of love-sicken behaviour can be identified with the ID factor which is very rare and strange in the case of women depicted in the *akam* poetry. The other types of women, usually of "adoptive behaviour," express their anger and pitiable condition when their husbands are determined to go out for gaining wealth. As a consequence of their attitude, they willfully blame their spouses; condemn them as people mad after materials. See in the poem what the woman told her friend on her husband's departure.[58]

> If it be strength
> to shake off love and kindness
> and depart in pursuit of wealth
> leaving us to languish,
> let him be strong.
> And let us womenfolk be
> fools in our fondness.
>
> (Kōpperuñcōlaṉ, *Kuṟuntogai* 20,
>   tr. Thangappa 2010:7)

This is a predominant behaviour of women who give vent to their anguish, hopelessness, pitiable situation when their husbands embark on a journey through the wilderness to an alien country. Since they are unable to dictate terms to their spouses against such missions, their behaviour shows their depression and underlying apathy in a sarcastic sense. They know that "working is life to men and men are life to women at home" (Pālai Pāḍiya Peruṅkaḍuṅkō, *KṞT* 135). "He is the life to my life. I cannot be away from him even for a wink," thus spells out a heroine to her *tōḻi* (Koṟṟaṉār, *KṞT* 218). Apparently, the women in *pālai* poems aware of the fact that their men must seek material wealth for leading the worldly life with comforts. But, at the bottom of their hearts—overtly they are afraid of hazards i.e., their men's safety in the wilderness and their subsequent safe return home but covertly they are worried over a unique threat i.e., their men's unfaithfulness of falling in love and marrying someone. While the wives doubt their husbands' integrity, their men usually assure them that they would not forsake them at any cost. The poem here paints a husband who reacts to his wife's doubting mind.[59]

O delicate young woman!

If I leave in this manner
and go away and stay
elsewhere abandoning
you,
causing your good heart
to suffer in loneliness,
may I suffer for many days
without anybody in need
coming to me requesting alms!

(Pālai Pāḍiya Peruṅkaḍuṅkō, *Kuṟuntogai* 137,
  tr. Vaidehi Herbert)[60]

The conflicting behaviour pattern i.e., "inner sphere" *vs*. "outer sphere" or "self" *vs*. "non-self" emerges from these poems. A man in *pālai*, in pre-marital or post-marital period, while thinking of going to an alien place, seriously weighs options whether to go away or not, naturally hesitates to decide. Being the bread winner of his home/family, it is a must for him to earn money, but he is caught between his sensuous heart and the pragmatic mind. The following poems amply show the "indecisive minds" of heroes which ultimately seem to be inclined in favour of their wives.[61]

Our manliness, not slacking, goads us to
go to earn wealth, but our love stops it.
My broken heart that is caught between
these two is sad, like an ant in the
middle of a stick that is burning with flames
on both ends, unable to go to either side.

Will she be sad? She is pitiful!

Love to living is what beautiful life is to the
body. Separation from the precious young
woman is like death!

(Naraimuḍi Neṭṭimaiyār, *Akanāṉūṟu* 339,
  tr. Vaidehi Herbert)[62]

My heart is tied to my beloved
with dark hair hanging on her back
and pretty, kohl-rimmed eyes with
the color of attractive petals
of blue waterlily blossoms.
It tells me that I should go to her
and end her sorrow.

My intelligence tells me that I should
finish my business, since it will bring
sorrow and shame to me if I do not
do so, and that I should not
veer from my work, even a little bit.

I am caught between my heart
and intelligence,
like a twisted old rope that is pulled
on both ends by male elephants
with bright, lifted tusks.

Will my distressed body be ruined?

(Tēypurip Paḷaṅkayiṟṟaṉār, *Naṟṟiṇai* 284,
tr. Vaidehi Herbert)[63]

These poems reveal how the *pālai* heroes are virtually torn between leaving to earn money and staying with their beloveds and not having wealth. Though their "reasoning minds" say that they should go to earn wealth, it will be difficult not to go. Struggling in poverty would be hard (Peruntalai Cāttaṉār, *NRI* 262). So, often there exists a serious debate between their "emotive hearts" and "analytical minds." Such a dilemma of a newly married man debating with his heart is seen in the following poem:[64]

You think that those without
any wealth cannot give to
others or enjoy pleasures.

You are thinking firmly
about leaving to gather wealth.

But will the dark, beautiful
woman come with us, or
are you sending me by myself?

Tell me, my heart!

(Ugāykkuḍi Kiḻār, *Kuṟuntogai* 63,
  tr. Vaidehi Herbert)[65]

It is very clear that he does not wish to go away alone leaving his ladylove. Separating from her and going alone on a long path filled with rocks in the wasteland to earn wealth is not a wise decision. Resolving in favour of his beloved lady, often he abandons his mission. While admonishing his own heart on one such occasion, the hero clearly says, he is not ready to take up the mission. So, decisively he puts the ball in the court of his heart to be with him or not. "O my heart I am not leaving the pretty, dark young woman to go to the forest with long, forked paths and rocks" (Madurai Marudaniḷa Nāgaṉār, *ANU* 245); "If you wish to go past the forest ... with a desire to go like others, feeling that leaving is good, you are fit to leave, my heart. I am not going to leave, hurting the young woman ... even if I were given the prosperous, huge country" (Kallāḍaṉār, *ANU* 199), thus the heroes convey their decisive words. Another husband similarly expresses his love for the beautiful wife by not choosing earning wealth over her in the following poem.[66]

The daughter, given to me by
those from the forest with mountains,
her arms wide, waist thin,
young breasts large and pretty with
budding yellow spots,
is cure to me if I want to be healed,
and riches to me if I want wealth.

(Karuvūr Ōdañāṉiyār, *Kuṟuntogai* 71,
  tr. Vaidehi Herbert)[67]

When he leaves his beloved and goes through the wilderness seeking wealth out of compulsion, even then he used to think of her warm relationship. A husband shares his thoughts on wilderness of the *pālai* tract which involves hazards and threats. He speaks: "The wasteland is a harsh place, where *ugā* trees with dried trunks, the colour of a pigeon's back shower down coin-like berries, as fierce-eyed bandits climb on its branches to look out for travelers and peel its bark and chew to quench their desire for water. However, it will be a sweet place if I go there thinking of her chest with fine breasts, the girl whose loins are adorned with jewels made of gold and gems" (Uruttiraṉār, *KṚT* 274). Another hero of *pālai* poems sometimes settles the score with his "analytical mind" on a compromise pact: "If she (heroine) will join me and go on the long forest path, what you have desired to acquire fearlessly, will be good!" (Kāvirip Pūmpaṭṭiṉattuc Cēndaṅkaṇṇaṉār, *KṚT* 347).

As such no hero in *pālai* poems has ever enjoyed his venture or time when he sets out on his journey. Neither he marries someone, nor does he settle down at the new place as feared by his woman. Largely the *pālai* poems caricature the dismal mood of lovers'/husbands' and their stupidity. Obviously, they think of their ladyloves who are far away during their mission. As seen earlier, either implicitly or explicitly they scold their mind/heart for all the miseries that they face. A hero in a *pālai* poem even goes to the extent of declaring that his decision to stay at home with his wife is wise but others are stupid: "I am embracing the chest of the delicate natured lady with fragrant, fine forehead and thick, dark hair. They are pitiable for all times, and without graces, those who are stupid to part from their sweet partners to earn new wealth" (Madurai Āciriyar Nallanduvaṉār, *ANU* 43).

The *pālai* theme (separation), seemingly the juxtaposed category of the *kuṛiñci* (union), in essence, comprises the poems that depict the more intense feeling of union. *Kuṟiñci* is basically the passion/crush between an "unknown boy and girl" which blossoms all of a sudden over their physical appearances and charming behaviours, slowly matures as "love" and ends with their "union" later. Whereas the *pālai*, "the separation" is another but arguably a continued phase of *kuṟiñci* in which "the lovers" knowing each other, either married or unmarried, get separated only to be united later. **When passion lurks in *kuṟiñci*, true love strives in *pālai*.** The former is more concerned with "body" and the latter with the "heart" or the "soul." So, the lover in *kuṟiñci* struggles all the while passing through tall mountainous and wild forest passages in the dead of night only to get united physically than emotionally with his ladylove at any cost. Whereas the lover or husband struggles all the more while passing through wild tracts filled with rocks and wild animals in the wasteland under the scorching sun at midday only to get united emotionally than physically with his beloved or wife at any cost. Perhaps, *kuṟiñci* and *pālai* can be understood as two poles positioned apart at different locations in a full circle but eventually meet at the same point. When *kuṟiñci* denotes the lover's "inward mobility" aimed more at the "exterior body," *pālai* is "outward mobility" aimed essentially at "interior heart"/"inner soul." In both *kuṟiñci* and *pālai*, the heroine is depicted frequently with the mood of anxiety. Her anxiety in *kuṟiñci* is concerned with the physical safety of the lover (who regularly meets her clandestinely at nights) as well as apprehension about his real intention of relationship. In *pālai*, her anxiety is explicit worry over her lover's or husband's physical safety while passing through wilderness and consequently concerned with his safe home coming at the same time implicitly apprehensive about his possible unfaithfulness. While the heroes in *kuṟiñci* poems show their enthusiasm and excitement in meeting their beloveds secretly, they openly express their empathy, compassion and caring attitude towards their sweethearts while seeking wealth in the wilderness of *pālai*. In a nutshell, it may be said that the heroes and heroines depicted in *pālai* theme predominantly represent the people of "adoptive behaviour but with conflicting interests" i.e., "home" *vs.* "house" or "emotive concern" *vs.* "economic motives."

"While *akam* and *puṟam*, and the five landscape genres, are opposed to each other as overall genres, and clearly defined as such, within each poem they work as phases, change points. One might even think of the action of each poem as a crossing of thresholds, across genres; the above *pālai* poem crosses from the outer landscape to the interior one, and also from the wilderness to the human settlement. Each of the genres enacts a characteristic crossing of the *akam/puṟam* oppositions. Typically, the movement of *akam* poems is a crossing from outer to inner; from outer body to the heart within, in memory or imagination (*kuṟiñci*); from sea to land (*neytal*), from war-field to home (*mullai*); from home to wilderness in actuality, from wilderness to home in memory (*pālai*); from the concubine who is no kin, who lives on the town's outskirts, to home, wife and kin (*marutam*)" (Ramanujan, *Op. cit.*, p. 265).

Assertive Behaviour of *Tōḻi*s (Confidantes) and *Pulavar*s (Poets/Bards) in *Akam* and *Puṟam* Poems

Next to the aesthetic depiction of heroes and heroines mostly picturised with "adoptive behaviour" in the Sangam poems, the other personae depicted so amusingly with the other type of "assertive behaviour" are *tōḻi*s, the confidantes of heroines and *pulavar*s (generally poets and sometimes the bards in specific contexts). "The bards, wandering "tribal encyclopedias," custodians and transmitters of past history, present science and prophetic knowledge, carry the good name of good men into the future as well as to others, and present the hero to himself" (*Ibid.*, p. 290). Though these personae represent the same type of behaviour, strikingly they are different in nature with varying interest. *Tōḻi*s who appear almost in the entire *akam* poems, represent the "interior world" whereas the poets/bards the "exterior world." The former are the dramatic personae (exclusively women) in *akam* poetry, the dearest friends of the heroines. The latter are non-dramatic personae (men or women) in *puṟam* poetry, known for their wisdom, audacity and integrity. They may be branded as "men of intelligence, peace makers, and advisors" who impress others with their "shrewd minds" and "dignified behaviours." Simply they are "the men of nobility with no self-interest." Sometimes, a set of them function as an acquaintance of heroes. They mediate between the sulking wife and the unfaithful husband who seeks entry into his home after spending the night at the concubine's house. Whereas as stated earlier, *tōḻi* is the daughter of the foster-mother, very sensible, pragmatic, truthful, gentle, caring, warm, thoughtful, and lifelike to the heroines. Always she conducts herself wholly in the interest of her friend. Being the woman persona so close to the heroine, she impeccably understands the latter's delicate feelings as well as her essential yearnings at critical situations. She just speaks and behaves as the "soul" or "conscience" of the latter in every situation. She is the sole mediator between the heroine and others (hero, bard, charioteer, foster-mother and biological mother) on lovesickness and other problems/issues of her friend. She intimately knows what is really good for both the hero and the heroine, and so she amply suggests, advises, encourages, soothes, and at times admonishes them while fixing their shortcomings.

It is quite natural that after some years of married-life, aged wives become "not-so-charming" to their husbands. The spouses, who are once adored as the delightful damsels/deer/peacocks so beautiful and dazzling, naturally lose their charm especially after bearing children. Their physical beauty lessens over the years.

They also lose interest in making themselves attractive to their husbands by not decking themselves with fragrant flowers, colourful dresses, and glittering ornaments. Having become disgruntled with the physical beauty as well as the reduced sexual appeal of their wives, usually the married men, as depicted in Sangam poems, develop extramarital relationship with charming, beautiful young women. Ridiculing their improper behaviour dictated by "sexual impulses and drives," the *tōḻi*s, though of the same age, assert themselves as responsible and thoughtful elders who have lived a full life. They approach their friends' personal delicate issues with utmost decency and handle the men of "impoverished behaviour" with proper understanding. The following poem presents a *tōḻi* as she pragmatically advises the hero (who is newly married to her friend) who plans to go away in search of wealth leaving his young wife.[68]

> O lord of the town laden with flowers!
> Even if her lifted, full breasts sag
> and even if her sapphire-colored hair
> draping on the back of her golden body
> turns grey, please do not abandon her!
>
> She understands clearly your faultless
> words that are like the unfailing spears
> of Palaiyan of Pōor who owns elephants
> with white tusks,
> who helped the victorious Chōzhas owning
> sweet, strong toddy and decorated chariots,
> to suppress the people of Kongu country.

(Unknown Poet, *Naṟṟiṇai* 10, tr. Vaidehi Herbert)[69]

Like a close senior family relative to the hero, the *tōḻi* advises him to take care of her friend in the coming days. It seems the couple is just married. It is typical that the elderly people who attend the wedding usually greet the couple to live long together. But it is too delicate, a greeting that only a *toli* can render. She anticipates that someday the hero may become disenchanted by the beauty of her friend. But she knows that her friend, newly married to him after some days of courtship, puts her total faith in him. The *tōḻi* sensibly conveys her friend's complete trust to him. Thereby she earnestly seeks him to be equally committed to her expectations. Directly but elegantly, she asks him not to forsake her friend even when her charm becomes less in the days to come. The message that she wants to convey to him is given in good spirits. She does it with firmness but in a pleasing manner. Her "assertive behaviour"—filled with sagacity, motherly affection, and sensible words—portrays her as a lovely darling at the end for both the hero and the heroine.

Considering them as her own children, she treats the hero and the heroine (her friend) with the equal affection, courtesy and thoughtfulness. This is what gets amply reflected in the following poem. A hero habitually meets his ladylove in the dead of night. He comes regularly swimming through vast marshes with shoals braving the murderous crocodiles. He has not yet thought of marrying his beloved. His thrilling visit and insensitive attitude irk the heroine as it does the *tōḻi*. Worried equally over the physical safety of the hero and mental sorrow of the heroine, the friend expresses her agony (over the clash between "body" and "heart") in a rare gesture—as "the mother anguished over her twins who ate poison"—explicitly in the poem following:[70]

> You
> come here because
> of your love for her,
>
> braving murderous male
> crocodiles with crooked
> legs, that cut off traffic,
> and swimming through
> vast backwaters with shoals
> of fish, near the vast seashore

with groves.
She
in her naive way is distressed.

And I
am terrified in my heart, like
a mother whose twins ate poison.

(Kavai Maganār, *Kuruntogai* 324,
   tr. Vaidehi Herbert)[71]

Seriously concerned with the well-being of both, she specifically conveys her terrified feeling arising out of his visits at the dead of night. Thereby, she indirectly suggests to him to marry the heroine at the earliest in the interest of saving the heroine from mental suffering. Her "pure mind" and "dignified behaviour" sweat for their benefit i.e., "home making" in essence. It may be stated that **no *tōḻi*s is portrayed as unconcerned or eccentric or hothead dramatis persona in any of the *akam* poems**.

A similar type of behaviour can be seen in every poem uttered by a poet or a bard. These men of intellect known for their integrity always work for the welfare of society. Though they struggle in penury, usually they never aspire for any gift or wealth from anyone. Such are their dignity and decency. If they see any unfairness or wrongdoing, they do not hesitate to point out those flaws. This set of people with a humanistic perspective feel that by generating shame and guilt in the perpetrators' minds for their wrongdoing and guiding them to a better sense, their negative mindset can be altered. So, they do counsel even kings on several occasions by risking their own life. This is their typical behaviour. These poets/bards of high esteem, as men of virtue/nobility in all respects, represent the behavioural pattern of "Super Ego" as classified by Sigmund Freud. There are countless such poets/bards who act purely in the interest of others, sometimes to save people and land, sometimes to highlight values and ethos, sometimes to unite estranged wife and husband and at times even cousins.

These poets, courageous by conviction, do excellent service for the cause of humanity. Once, a Cōḻa king Kuḷamuṟṟattut Tuñciya Kiḷḷivaḷavaṉ conquers his enemy Malaiyamāṉ in the battle. After eliminating him, he imprisons his little children along with others and brings them to his country only to kill them cruelly. In a public place, where numerous people have gathered, he buries them alive, leaving only their heads above the pits to allow the elephants to trample them under foot. Coming to know about the imminent inhuman action, the poet Kōvūr Kiḻār enters the scene at the right moment to save the innocent children. He counsels the brutal king with courage and conviction. Listen to the concerned voice of the poet:[72]

> You come from the line of Cōḻa king
> who gave his flesh
> for a pigeon in danger,
>   and for others besides,
> and these children also come
> from a line of kings
> who in their cool shade
> share all they have
>
> lest poets,
> those tillers of nothing
> but wisdom,
> should suffer hardships.
>
> Look at these children,
> the crowns of their heads are still soft.
>
> As they watch the elephants,
> they even forget to cry,
> stare dumbstruck at the crowd
> in some new terror
> of things unknown.

> Now that you've heard me out,
> do what you will.
>
> (Kōvūr Kiḻār to Kiḷḷi Vaḷavaṉ, *Puranāṉūṟu* 46,
>   tr. Ramanujan 1985:122)

The kindhearted poet, worried about the life of children, does not hesitate to counsel his king when he feels that the latter's action is unjust. In the realm of politics, it is quite natural, fitting and justifiable that one finishes off one's opponents. "For a man to be defeated or slain by another man is the nature of this world" (Iḍaikkuṉṟūr Kiḻār to Pāṇḍiyaṉ Talaiyālaṅkāṉattuc Ceruveṉṟa Neḍuñceḻiyaṉ, *PNU* 76). The self-protecting drive motivates a person to eliminate his/her opponent by any means for survival. Especially, it is more warranted to the kings/chieftains to destroy their enemies wholly with their wives and children. Obviously, therefore they cannot be merciful. If they show them any lenience, then their own lives and the survival of their kith and kin, clan, and other people would be in peril. Surely, they would perish in a matter of time. But for noble men, these reasons are out of reach. No matter who the others are, all humans are one community for them, irrespective of creed, colour, profession, gender, and age. Driven by the sentiments of "Super Ego" (man consciously elevating himself to high position by nurturing divine qualities), i.e., "soul" *vs.* "body," the poet tries to win the "heart" of the cruel king by expressing his "super soul." This is overtly to save the "physical bodies" of enemies' children but covertly concerned for their "psyche" or "soul" (inner self) in essence. The "assertive behaviour" of the poet who conducts himself with no desire for personal gain and in a cool manner, indeed, wins over the king at the end. One sees here, the "graceful, tactful, intelligent mind" (Super Ego) as it wins the "ordinary mind" (ID) driven by the "impulses and drives of self-protecting aggressive behaviour."

In another poem,[73] the same poet Kōvūr Kiḻār, with the same conviction, counsels two estranged cousins all set for battle. The poet, who truly seeks peace between Neḍuṅkiḷḷi and Nalaṅkiḷḷi, the warring cousins, places the hard reality before them to consider for their own interest and that of their families as follows:

> Your enemy is not the kind who wears
> the white leaf of the tall palmyra
>
> nor the kind who wears garlands
> from the black-branched neem trees.
>
> Your chaplets are made of laburnum,
> your enemies are made of laburnum too.
>
> When one of you loses
> the family loses,
>
> and it is not possible
> for both to win.
>
> Your ways show no sense of family:
> they will serve only to thrill
> alien kings
>
>> whose chariots are bannered,
>> like your own.

(Kōvūr Kiḻār to Neḍuṅkiḷḷi and Nalaṅkiḷḷi,
Puranāṉūṟu 45, tr. Ramanujan 1985:121)

Though the poet counsels them for their personal and people's welfare yet neither heeds his words. Nalaṅkiḷḷi besieges the palace of Neḍuṅkiḷḷi and hides himself there. Neither does he surrender, nor does he fight. By his inaction everything is in a mess, and people suffer most. Irked by his inaction, the poet becomes irritated. Hence once again, he intervenes and admonishes Nalaṅkiḷḷi. In the following poem, he spells out his reasons:[74]

The male elephants cannot go to the huge reservoirs
to bathe with their females, nor have they been fed
mashed rice mixed with ghee, and so they lean on
their strong posts with perfect bases, bending them,
distressed, their trunks rolling on the ground as they
sigh with hot breaths and trumpet like thunder.

Babies scream without milk, women tie their bare
hair without flowers and wailing sounds are heard
from fine, well-constructed houses that have no water.
It is cruel for you to linger here, O Greatness with
powerful horses whose strengths are hard to measure!
If you are righteous, open the gates and tell him
that it is his. If you live by martial laws, open and fight!
If you are without righteousness or martial courage
and just hide on one side within your high walls,
your door with sturdy headers closed, it is cause for shame!

(Kōvūr Kiḻār to Neḍuṅkiḷḷi, *Puranāṉūṟu* 44,
   tr. Vaidehi Herbert)[75]

The ways in which the poet speaks, advises and admonishes the chieftains/kings have been well taken in good spirit by one and all. In fact, "the poets were the articulate bearers of honour and blame, and so they had the power to counsel, to sneer and curse, and to make peace and to point to the vanity of human, even royal, wishes. They were the censors and mirrors, the memories and superegos of the heroic milieu" (Ramanujan, *Ibid.*, p. 291).

Poets like Kōvūr Kiḻār intervene, counsel, and at times admonish kings, and chieftains not only on public matters of the state but also on their personal/private matters. A chieftain called Pēgaṉ[76] starts living with another woman leaving his wife Kaṇṇagi in distress. He is very generous at making poets/bards immensely happy with his lavish gifts. Once he drapes a peacock with his shawl out of compassion, thinking it would shiver in the cold during monsoon season (Paraṇar, *PNU* 141 & 142). Coming to know about his unfaithfulness to his wife, the poets such as

Paraṇar, Kabilar, Aricil Kiḻār and Peruṅkuṉṟūr Kiḻār voice their concern and disapproval, though separately, but they all join on one issue. "Who is that pitiable woman unable to hold back her flowing tears, her breasts wet, and she cried constantly, sounding like a sad flute" (Kabilar, *PNU* 143), "It is cruel that you don't show any compassion to a young woman in great grief" (Paraṇar, *PNU* 144), "The gift I beg from you is that you mount your tall chariot strung with bells and remove the anguish of your wife. Please show compassion!" (Paraṇar, *PNU* 145), "We do not want your wealth or precious jewels. May that stay with you! If you want to give me a gift, then please hitch your fast horses to your tall cha-riot, and go to your young wife wearing fine jewels, in great despair, wasting away through your cruelty" (Aricil Kiḻār, *PNU* 146), "Grant me the gift of you going to your wife today, the beautiful dark woman, who yesterday, stood alone in despair" (Peruṅkuṉṟūr Kiḻār, *PNU* 147), thus they all express their grief to the great Pēgaṉ in unison. Though it is the delicate, personal matter of the chieftain and his wife, these poets do not hesitate to advise and admonish him. As these great poets are really concerned about the blissful family life, they voluntarily speak their hearts only to see the chieftain and his wife united. This is a kind of typical "Super Ego" behaviour through which one can understand the function of the "Conscious mind of Superhuman beings" like these poets with impeccable character.

Sometimes these noble souls, as great friends of chieftains/ kings don't mind to die with them as their friendship is very emotional. A poet/bard Picirāndaiyār, the great friend of Kōpperuñ-cōlaṉ whom he has never met before, carries out this extraordinary/unbelievable act. The king has problems with his own sons who rise up in arms against him. He feels that they have disgraced his lineage. So, he sits facing north, starves himself to death. Along with him sit his great soul mate Picirāndaiyār and other poets, facing north and starve themselves to death (Kōpperuñcōlaṉ, *PNU* 214–16). Behind this "Super Behaviour" of the noble poets, there stands out the "Super Ego" that spurs them to join the king even in death. These poets are the people who once hugely enjoyed the largesse of the generous king. Now they desire to re-pay their debt by joining him at death and thus showing their soli-darity. This is the virtue that they consider as more important than their own lives. What they seek is a good name (*naṟpeyar*), hon-our (*pugaḻ*) in life or in the death no shame (*nāṇ*) or blame (*paḻi*) in their private and public life. That is why, the king Cēramāṉ Peruñcēralādaṉ (known for his martial courage and skill) also chooses to die facing north but for other reasons as he takes a wound on his back when he is defeated by the Cōḻa king Kari-kālaṉ at Veṇṇi battlefield (Kaḻāttalaiyār, *PNU* 65). In a similar fashion, another king also does the same but for a different rea-son. The king Cēramāṉ Kaṇaikkāl Irumpoṟai is once defeated by the Coḻaṉ Ceṅkaṇṇāṉ at Kaḻumalam battle. He is imprisoned, put into a small cell and is ill-treated. Feeling thirsty, he asks for a glass of water. Least bothered about his request, a soldier brings water after much delay. Feeling utterly sad about the ill-treatment, he refuses to quench his thirst and eventually dies without sipping even a drop of water. Before his death, he himself has uttered the following poem in which his "Super Ego" is adeptly demonstra-ted.[77]

> If an infant died or if a fetus was born as a mass of flesh,
> even though they were not adults, my ancestors,
> treated them as such and cut them with swords. It has
> now come to this, and I'm sitting here suffering like a
> dog in chains, not cut up like a hero, without any mental
> strength, and having to plead for water to enemies without
> generosity, to calm down the fire in my stomach. Do parents
> in royal families bear children in this world for this? No!
>
> (Cēramāṉ Kaṇaikkāl Irumpoṟai *Puranāṉūru* 74,
> tr. Vaidehi Herbert)[78]

Aggressive Behaviour of Women/Warriors/Chieftains/ Kings in *Akam* and *Puṟam* Poems

The heroes and the heroines are shown to exhibit "adoptive behaviour." The *tōḻi*s and poets/bards are largely depicted under the category of "assertive behaviour." There are other personae such as warriors, chieftains and kings who fit into the last category i.e., "aggressive behaviour." These people may be identified as the personae of "dark minds"—"people who brutally kill innocent men, women and children to prove a point, individuals who destroy fellow human beings to fulfil their misplaced desires" (Pulkit Sharma, *Speaking Tree*).[79] "It has been postulated that males behave differently from women because of their differing roles from prehistoric times. Man, the hunter, had of necessary to be aggressive and adventurous. Woman, the gatherer, developed competence in collecting and preserving what was needed for daily living and in developing a home. These differing skills were then passed on through the genes that go into creating a boy or a girl" (Pandya, *Op. cit.*, p. 78). Ancient Indian scriptures categorise men into three kinds namely *sattva* ("purity and light," sages, intellectuals etc.), *rajas* ("passion and activity," *kshatria*s, ruling class) and *tamas* ("inertia and darkness" or "dullness," service/ working/low castes) on the basis of their *guṇa*s and behaviour.[80] If *sattva* dominates the mind, it becomes one-pointed and the seeker enters into a meditative mood spontaneously; if *tamas* dominates, the mind is enveloped by darkness and loses its power of discrimination; and if *rajas* holds sway, the mind hankers after power, position and prestige and becomes overambitious.[81]

The *Bhagavad Gita* in the seventeenth chapter explains how these *guṇa*s manifest in us: *Sattva*: Being immaculate is illuminating and flawless and leads to joy and wisdom. *Rajas*: Passion results in longing and attachment, motivating the individual to action and to face the consequences. *Tamas:* Ignorance deludes through negligence, inactivity, laziness, and sleep. So, the man who approaches his fellows and all beings with pure love and kindness, who wishes to develop divine qualities and sees divinity in everything is identified with *satvik* behaviour. The man who approaches his fellow beings with likings and dislikings based on reasons signifies *rajasik*. The person who approaches his/her counterparts with jealousy and enmity is *tamasik*. While *sattva* indicates the people of "assertive behaviour," the *tamas* arguably denotes the people of "adoptive behaviour." The middle category *rajas* seemingly refers to the people of "aggressive behaviour."

No one, allegedly, can be said to be aggressive in his/her birth itself. Arguably, "some degree of aggression is essential to survival and progress. The infant that will not bawl its head off when hungry may not get its feed. The mother who does not guard her offspring forcefully may see them carried off by predators. Without such a drive we would be unable to conquer difficulties or explore the world or, indeed, ward off cruel behaviour. It is when aggression is aimed at subjugating, injuring, torturing and destroying others that it assumes reprehensible overtones. The fight response (with the alternative possibility of flight), integral to aggressive behaviour, is built mammalian systems and developed as a protective mechanism" (*Ibid.*, pp. 111–12).

Pathologically, "a malfunctioning mind results in abnormal behaviour" (*Ibid.*, p. 4). As observed by Behaviourists, one's cognizance, capability and the given environment alone can determine a person's behaviour. In the 'Heroic Age,' men apparently lived in dangerous environments. The hazards were partly natural (poisonous reptiles, wild animals, furious rain, gushing floods, grave coldness, fire, etc.) and partly humans (murders, assassinations, wars, etc.). In order to protect himself, man began to attack the other. In 'Stone Age' and its subsequent historical periods, negative sentiments like threat, impatience, anger, jealousy, struggle, frustration, annoyance, antagonism, intimidation, etc., were strong and manifested in the psyche of human beings than positive ones. Naturally, negative attributes were reflected in the behaviour of human beings as depicted in the poems of Sangam classics which belong to the 'Heroic Age.'

Abnormal Behaviour of Heroines at the Loss of their Spouses in *Puṟam* Poems

Indian women usually suppress their feelings, whether it is happiness or anger or frustration, or any sentiment since historical age as they have been constantly under the oppression of men. Contrary to this, an *akam* poem presents the heroine, caught in her love feelings, as throwing herself into the flames against her own village people who do not show any concern for her suffering. She is very frustrated, probably since her lover/husband has left her to earn wealth. She does not know how to handle her painful lovesickness. How she furiously gives vent to her anger is seen in the following poem:[82]

> Will I hit them? Will I attack them?
> Will I scream 'Ah' and 'Ol' citing
> some reason?
> The swirling wind blows and causes
> me distress, while those in this town
> are sleeping, unaware of my love
> affliction.
>
> I do not know what to do!
>
> (Avvaiyār, *Kuṟuntogai* 28, tr. Vaidehi Herbert)[83]

This is perhaps the only poem which depicts the utter painful lovesickness of a heroine to her friend. In the vocabulary of Clinical Psychology her outburst could be identified with the term "hysteria."[84] Since women are subjected to suppression/intimidation every time and everywhere, their suppressed feelings burst out at times against men-folk or society. Suppression of one's emotive feelings is, indeed, like a rice cooker withstanding the pressure for some reasonable time. Men always have ways to release their pressure through some means but the same is culturally forbidden for women since ages. This is perhaps reflected in the behaviour of the heroine in the poem. A woman poet namely Ādimandi who seems to be similarly affected but not exactly in the same manner, also outbursts like the earlier heroine. She searches for her husband Āṭṭanatti, a warrior cum an accomplished dancer, on his sudden desertion. It seems that she has just married him against the wishes of her family members. Naturally, she is upset over the unfortunate development. She searches for him everywhere but unsuccessfully. So, she proudly declares in the following poem:[85]

> I cannot find my esteemed man
> among warriors at their festival,
> nor with the women who hug and
> perform *tuṇaṅgai* dance.
>
> I am a dancer whose love for him
> has made my bright conch shell
> bangles slip off my wasting hands.
>
> My proud lover is a dancer too.
>
> (Ādimandi, *Kuṟuntogai* 31, tr. Vaidehi Herbert)[86]

One could see how a woman's psyche, affected by her husband's sudden desertion, becomes so daring to forsake the inhibition of her womanhood. Thereby she declares publicly that the untraceable person is her man. Perhaps, she deliberately wants to convey her relationship with the man whom she has wedded earlier to her family members and society.

There is another strange, but the most painful "self-annihilating behaviour" found in the conduct of women (psychologically depressed and abysmal) in those days—that is *sati* (wife entering into the burning pyre with the body of her husband), an irrational custom practiced till the advent of the Britishers in India. In this cruel custom, a queen namely Peruṅkōppeṇḍu earnestly desires to end her life in front of her relatives and people. She is unable to withstand the irreparable loss of her husband Ollaiyūr Tanda Bhūdappāṇḍiyaṉ who died leaving her in great distress. She is so depressed, according to the then existing culture as she wants to enter the funeral pyre along with the body of her husband despite requests to rule the country. "Abandoning her youth, she with large, distressed eyes, walked toward the burning pyre in the vast ground, she whose sweet life would tremble if she were to be away from her husband even for a short while, in their well-guarded huge palace where drums never stop" (Maduraip Pērālavāyar to Bhūdappāṇḍiyaṉ wife Peruṅkōppeṇḍu, *PNU* 247). She is from an ancient clan and is politically astute, yet she does not wish to live anymore for obvious reasons. The main reason is personal. So, being very emotional at the unbearable loss of her husband's death, she becomes deeply depressed. Another reason is historical. During the 'Herioc Age,' the widows of enemy kings are taken as slaves, illtreated and also sexually exploited by the kings who win the war. Fearing such fate, she might have ended her life. By her act, it is perceived as to how a situation determines one's mind to function in a certain way.

Demonic Behaviour of Kings while conquering Neighbour Countries

Chieftains/Kings, who are immensely eulogized for their generosity and compassion, indeed, have other distinctive behaviour too. Their "aggressive behaviour," impelled by arrogance, annoyance, intolerance, greed, etc., often obliterates their enemies as well as their countries leaving them in a dismantled condition without getting them restored. While enacting their attack on the enemy kings, either compelled by the notion of self-defense or the various counterattacks, they never feel rued in destroying other's land and water resources and killing the innocent people savagely. In the quest of protecting their land and people, usually the chieftains/kings breach the lines of righteousness. There are numerous poems which praise "the heroic behaviour of the chieftains/kings of high esteem" while a few condemn it. Look at the following heroic poem:[87]

On the streets of your enemy countries dug up by your
fast chariots, you yoked dull colored donkeys with
with white-mouths and plowed their protected vast spaces.
You rode your chariot across their land, and the curved
hooves of your horses, galloping with their white plumes
furrowed their famed, fertile fields where flocks of birds
sing. You ruined their guarded ponds with your elephants
with enraged looks, huge swaying necks, wide feet, and
gleaming tusks.

Given your rage, which one of these is greater in number
– the eager enemy foot soldiers who retreated in shame
and live with blame, after they came with a desire to
ruin your strength, brandishing their tall spears that
throw shadows and beautiful shields made with bright iron,
to fight against your army with shining weapons, or
the number of huge fields where you have planted columns
after performing faultless rituals prescribed by the four good
Vedas, with precious sacrificial elements and abundant ghee?

O Greatness, your valor is the proper theme for songs that
celebrate invasions, performed by women singers to the beats
of drums smeared with clay and tied tightly with leather strips!

(Neṭṭimaiyār to Pāṇḍiyaṉ Palyāgacālai Mudukuḍumip
Peruvaḻudi, *Puranāṉūṟu* 15, tr. Vaidehi Herbert)[88]

Thus, the poet Neṭṭimaiyār praises Pāṇḍiyaṉ Palyāgacālai Mudukuḍumip Peruvaḻudi's heroic deeds. He conveniently portrays his every "demonic behaviour"—destroying enemy's lands, orchards, and ponds etc.—with a positive mind-set. When many poets usually stand for compassion, humanity and good governance, some of them strangely picturise the negative conduct of kings as positive. "You do not consider whether it is day or nights to plunder enemy towns, blazing them as their citizens cry loudly. O Vaḷavaṉ riding your elegant chariot! There is nothing remaining in your enemy countries where there were prosperous towns, where, instead of mud, they used fish to block holes of dams with sounds of cool flowing water!" (Karuṅkuḻal Ādaṉār to Cōḻaṉ Karikāl Peruvaḷattāṉ, *PNU* 7), "Your limitless army advances in the field, ruins rich fields, baths elephants in their guarded reservoirs and destroys enemy lands. The light from the fires lit with the wood in houses, appears like the red glow of the sun as it folds down its rays. O Lord who is as fierce as Murugaṉ! You lit bright flames in their protected lands, devastating huge, lovely fields" (Pāṇḍaraṅkaṇṇaṉār to Cōḻaṉ Rājacūyam Vēṭṭa Perunarkiḷḷi, *PNU* 16), "You are like the sun that rises from the sea, never relenting in your fierce rage toward your enemies, but like the moon to people like me" (Maduraik Kūlavāṇigaṉ Cīttalaic Cāttaṉār to Pāṇḍiyaṉ Cittiramāḍattut Tuñciya Naṉmāṟaṉ, *PNU* 59).

Contrary to hailing the kings' heroic deeds, a poet namely Māṟōkkattu Nappacalaiyār slights a king as follows: "O heir of Cembiyaṉ who removed the anguish of a dove and owned a rage-filled army with bright spears ... You attacked like roaring thunder. You have the skill to ruin this great ancient city. Great leader! Without considering this as wondrous, you are able to destroy with great strength in battle!" (Māṟōkkattu Nappacalaiyār to Cōḻaṉ Kuḻamuṟṟattut Tuñciya Kiḷḷivaḷavaṉ, *PNU* 37). But, the poet Neṭṭimaiyār, who praises Pāṇḍiyaṉ Palyāgacālai Mudukuḍumip Peruvaḻudi for his heroic deeds earlier, however, with a change of mind/heart for some unknown reasons, later spurns the same king openly as follows: "O victorious noble Kuḍumi! Is this fair? You seize land from others and do sweet things for those who ask for favours. You give gold lotuses for bards to wear and elephants with ornamented brows along with decorated chariots for poets to mount" (Neṭṭimaiyār to Pāṇḍiyaṉ Palyāgacālai Mudu-kuḍumip Peruvaḻudi, *PNU* 12). Thus, the poets' minds deliver two different judgments in the same given period. The dichotomy seems to be varying because of "environmental sentiment" *vs.* "individual consciousness." Personally no one—particularly, poets who strive sincerely for humanity—would ever welcome or encourage any action whatsoever like someone destroying the other, nature or environment. Perhaps it could be a case of the clash between the "individual mind" and "social mind" of the by-gone era.

Magaṭpāṟ Kāñci (War ensuing from seeking a Girl in Marriage): Aggressive Behaviour of the Ancient Tamiḻ Kings

A peculiar "aggressive behaviour of the ancient Tamiḻ kings" known as *makaṭpāṟ kāñci*, (lit. *makaḷ* = daughter, *pāl* = related/through, *kāñci* = impermanence), refusing to give daughter in marriage to kings) is vividly described in several *puṟam* poems (in *Puranāṉūṟu* alone 21 poems—336 through 356) in a way reminiscent of "the extreme behaviour of hotheads." It describes very strange situations where the three mighty Tamiḻ kings (Kings from Cēra, Cōḻa, Pāṇḍiya dynasties) come for the hands of girls from ancient clans, which refuse to give their daughters in marriage. When they are confronted, the fathers and brothers of the girls fight with their weapons and chase away the suitors. The suitors cause terrible damage to the towns. The people then live constantly in fear. Genuine feelings and nice gestures from unfriendly kings are invariably doubted. The desire for "self-protection" or "expanding the territory of the kingdom" often drives the chieftains/kings to wage war on some pretext or other.

In the ancient Tamil̲ culture, it seems, marriages between adults took place only after their courtship. Perhaps no conventional/traditional marriage systems arranged by parents existed. When the kings from the three great dynasties formally ask for the hand of a beautiful girl from an ancient clan, they are snubbed for some reasons. Because they do not approach the girl's parents (who are already in animosity) in a pleasing manner. Very strangely, battles take place at the formal request of the kings who wish to marry the girl with her parents' permission. Such battles and devastations often take place because of the animosity that prevails already in the psyche of the kings, girls, their parents and brothers. Kings, as they are monarchs, speak harshly to the fathers of girls. Their "authoritative behaviour" irks everyone. As a result, the marriage does not take place, but battle ensues. The following poem depicts this aspect:[89]

> The king wipes the sweat from his forehead with the tip
> of his spear and speaks harshly. Her father just utters
> big words without being humble. This is their policy.
> When analyzing, it appears that this dark, pretty, young
> woman with sharp teeth and moist, lovely eyes with red
> lines, has become a terror to this town where she was
> born, like a small fire lit by kindling that burns down the
> log on which the fire is started!
>
> (Madurai Marudani̲la Nāga̲nār, *Pu̲ranā̲nū̲ru* 349,
> tr. Vaidehi Herbert)[90]

The body language of the king is well described in the poem. The king wipes the sweat from his forehead with the tip of his spear and also speaks harshly. This is just enough for the father of the girl who is already in a hostile mood to fight. As the following literary evidences from Sangam classics suggest, no one, either from the kings' side or from the girls' side really wishes to have matrimonial relationship. It seems that they want to settle their old enmity in the guise of seeking alliance now. The related "antagonistic feelings" and "aggressive behaviours" are described in the poems as follows: "She will not agree if someone is unworthy of her even if they came humbly with abundant fine gifts. Also, her father will not give her in marriage" (Paraṇar, *PNU* 343), "If the three great victorious kings, wearing on their heads strands of neem, *ātti* and palm come with bows, but do not pay homage to him, he will not give his naïve daughter" (Kuṉṟūr Kiḻār, *PNU.* 338), "The father of the young girl will not give her to the king, even though he begs for her" (Paraṇar, *PNU* 341), "Even if the king starts a great war, he cannot get her. Her noble brothers pile corpses in tall heaps and plow daily with battle elephants as their bulls" (Aricil Kiḻār, *PNU* 342), "Her mighty brothers who confront and kill will not be satisfied without a battle" (Madurai Mēlaikkaḍaik Kaṇṇampuguttār Āyattaṉār, *PNU* 350), "Her brothers do not want wealth. They will not give her to any man who is not their equal. They desire to enter into battles" (Aḍaineḍum Kalviyār, *PNU* 345).

So, because of their animosity their ancient cities are ruined, and their people are killed. "Well protected ancient city has fallen into despair. It is sad" (Paraṇar, *PNU* 336), "Will the fine, large city suffer, since those who have come have placed ladders to force their way in, and sighing kites rest on the middle wall of the fort, the paths to it protected by warriors?" (Paraṇar, *PNU* 343), "With warriors as fierce as tigers, he will not be false to his vow. Filled with rage, he ordered his soldiers to wear flowers and bathe in a pond. Thereby the cool fertile city lost its great beauty like a cool pond ruined by warring bull elephants" (Paraṇar, *PNU* 341).

All these words invariably speak "the antagonistic feelings" and "haughty behaviours" that exist among the ancient clans of

Tamil̲ kings. This is the only category in which all personae have the same/alike "Aggressive" or "Rejecting Behaviour" only to suffer themselves as well as others. Their "aggressive behaviours" as such seem to be conditioned by their environmental situations of the 'Heroic Age' in which man sometimes behaves worse than demons.

It may be concluded that when we observe "the mind and conduct of different personae" as articulated in the poems of Sangam classics, certain kinds of "Behavioural Psychology" strikingly emanate in binary opposition. The way *akam* and *pur̲am*, the five landscape genres, and their themes are opposed to each other, the personae and their behaviours also to a greater extent differ fittingly to the demands of situations. As **women predominantly represent "the emotive heart," their behaviour strives hard for "home making" or "safeguarding family system" which is the cardinal point of *akam* poetry. On the contrary, men who predominantly represent "the analytical mind," driven by sensuous feelings and economic concern, at times sabotage the women's psyche. Thereby, they become representing "home breaking" or "sabotaging the family system."** *Tōl̲i*s and poets/bards as they duly represent *akam* and *pur̲am* ("interior world" *vs.* "exterior world") function as the conscience and caretakers of the heroine and the hero respectively. While the former is solely concerned about the well-being of the heroine, the latter is for society's well-being. As such both these categories have intelligence and noble attributes with no selfish agenda. As they are driven by the impulses of self-protection and expanding the boundaries of their territory, naturally chieftains/kings represent the people of "aggressive behaviour." **Interestingly every dramatis persona has a 'typical behaviour' as well as an 'atypical attitude.'**

Notes

1. *Eṭṭuttogai* (Eight Anthologies): *Naṟṟiṇai, Kuṟuntogai, Aiṅkuṟu-*
   ṇūṟu, Kalittogai, Akanāṇūṟu, Patiṟṟuppattu, Puṟanāṇūṟu, Pari-
   pāḍal.

   Pattuppāṭṭu (Ten Idylls or Ten Songs): *Kuṟiñcippāṭṭu, Maduraik-*
   kāñci, Porunar Āṟṟuppaḍai, Ciṟupāṇ Āṟṟuppaḍai, Perumpāṇ
   Āṟṟuppaḍai, Malaipaḍukaḍām, Mullaippāṭṭu, Neḍunalvāḍai,
   Paṭṭiṇappālai, Tirumurugu Āṟṟuppaḍai.

2. *Akam* poems are love poems; *puṟam* are all other kinds of poems,
   usually about war, values, community; it is the "public" poetry of
   the ancient Tamils, celebrating the ferocity and glory of kings, la-
   menting the death of heroes, the poverty of poets. Elegies, panegyr-
   ics, invectives, poems on wars and tragic events are *puṟam* poems.

   Only the full cycle of love between well-matched lovers is called
   akam; all else, including ill-matched love, the life and death of heroes, their relations to land, clan, enemy, and bard, were called
   puṟam (See: A.K. Ramanujan 1985:268).

3. *kāmam cālā iḷamai yōḷvayiṇ*
   ēmam cālā iḍumbai eydi
   naṇmaiyum tīmaiyum eṇṟiru tiṟattāl
   taṇṇoḍum avaḷoḍum tarukkiya puṇarttuc
   colledir peṟā-aṇ colli iṇbuṟal
   puḷḷit tōṇṟum kaikkiḷaik kuṟippē
   (Tolkāppiyam, Poruḷadigāram, Akattiṇai Iyal 50)

4. *ēriya maḍaṟṟiṟam iḷamai tīrtiṟam*
   tēṟudal oḷinda kāmattu migutiṟam
   mikka kāmattu miḍaloḍu togai-ic
   ceppiya nāṇgum peruntiṇaik kuṟippē
   (Tolkāppiyam, Poruḷadigāram, Akattiṇai Iyal 51)

5. *The Psychological Symbolism of Pālai in Kuruntokai* by Lalitha Sambamoorthy, in the Proceedings   of the Second International Conference/Seminar of Tamil Studies, Jan. 1968, ed. by R.E. Asher, International Association of Tamil Studies, Madras, 1971, pp. 25–33.

   Pālaikkaliyil Uḷaviyal (in Tamiḻ) by N. Paramasivam, Assistant Professor in Tamil, K.S.R. Arts and Science, Tirucenkodu, Namakkal District, Tamil Nadu State.
   (Source: http://Tamilparks.50webs.com/Tamilpoem/ulaveeyal_paramasivam.html).

   Peṇṇiya Uḷaviyal Nōkkil Veḷḷivīdiyār Pāḍalgaḷ, a critical essay written in Tamiḻ by Dr. M. Palaniyappan, Associate Professor in Tamiḻ, M. Mannar College, Pudukkottai, Tamil Nadu State.
   (Source: http://www.penniyam.com/2011/03/blog-post_26.html).

6. 'Psychology' is a term derived from the Greek words *'psyche'* and *'logos'*, meaning 'soul' and 'study'. To Greeks, Psychology is simply a study of the soul.

7. Steven Blankaart, P. 13 as quoted in "psychology n.", *A Dictionary of Psychology*, Edited by Andrew M. Colman, Oxford University Press, 2009, Oxford Reference Online, Oxford University Press, oxfordreference.com.
   (Source: http://en.wikipedia.org/wiki/Psychology).

8. Green, C.D. & Groff, P.R., 2003, *Early psychological thought: Ancient accounts of mind and soul*, Westport, Connecticut: Praeger.
   (Source: http://en.wikipedia.org/wiki/Psychology).

9. Brink, T.L., 2008, Psychology: A Student Friendly Approach, "Unit One: The Definition and History of Psychology", pp. 9. (Source: http://en.wikipedia.org/wiki/Psychology).

10. Source: http://en.wikipedia.org/wiki/Psychology.

11. Source: http://en.wikipedia.org/wiki/Psychology.

12. Source: http://en.wikipedia.org/wiki/Psychology.

13. Mandler, G., 2007, *A history of modern experimental psychology: From James and Wundt to cognitive science*, Cambridge, MA: MIT Prerss. (Source: http://en.wikipedia.org/wiki/Psychology).

14. Freud, S., 1900, *The Interpretation of Dreams, IV* and *V* (2nd Ed.), Hogarth Press, 1955 & Freud, S., 1915, *The Unconscious XIV* (2nd Ed.), Hogarth Press, 1955.
(Source: http://en.wikipedia.org/wiki/Psychology).

15. http://www.srmuniv.ac.in/Tamilperayam/Tamil_courses/Lessons/MA_Tamil/IV_Year/matt18/html/ mat18005uplg.htm

16. Some basic physiological and psychological drives:
   - Hunger Drive, a feeling of hunger motivates a person to look for food.
   - Thirst Drive, a feeling of thirst motivates a person to look for water/liquid to maintain water level in the body.
   - Sex Drive, a physical as well as psychological urge that stimulates a person to satisfy himself/herself by engaging in sexual acts.
   - Self-protecting Drive, a feeling of self-protection motivates a person to eliminate his/her opponent by any means for survival.

17. June 2008 study by the American Psychoanalytic Association, as reported in the *New York Times*, "Freud is Widely Taught at Universities, Except in the Psychology Department" by Patricia Cohen, November 25, 2007.

18. Overt: Behaviour that is observable by others and can be seen readily (ex. Laughing, shouting, talking, etc.)

19. Covert: Behaviour that is internal therefore not observable and cannot be seen. This comes in the forms of feelings, thoughts, and motives (ex. Happy, angry, imaginations, etc.).

20. Skinner, B.F., 1974, *About Behaviorism*, New York: Random House (Quoted: From Wikipedia, The Free Encyclopedia, "Psychology").

21. Overskeid, G., 2007, "Looking for Skinner and finding Freud", *American Psychologist* 62 (6), 590–595 (Quoted: From Wikipedia, The Free Encyclopedia, "Psychology").

22. Inner feelings of women: Ecstasy in sexual union (*kuṟiñci*), patient waiting for husband and happiness in marriage (*mullai*), sulking over the unfaithfulness of husband (*marudam*), anxious waiting for lover/husband who failed to return on the agreed period (*neydal*) and accepting the hard reality of separation of lover/husband who departs usually to take part in the army of kingdom on invasion or who frequently departs to alien country on business trip or who seldom departs away on academic agenda (*pālai*).

23. http://mhcd7.wordpress.com/2013/04/28/உளவியல்-நோக்கில்-காதல்/

24. *Tolkāppiyam*: The *Tolkāppiyam* is the earliest and most authoritative Tamiḻ grammar, an important work in Indian linguistics, and a text essential to any understanding of classical Tamiḻ poetry and culture. What Panini's grammar is to Sanskrit, the *Tolkāppiyam* is to Tamiḻ.

   Of its three sections, the first two (*eḻuttu* and *col*) deal with linguistic matters (orthography and phonology; morphology and syntax). The third section, on *poruḷ* or "substance, subject matter, meaning", deals with prosody, rhetoric, poetics, genres, themes, codes of behaviour, poetic diction, and cultural semantics. Like many other Indian expository texts, this work is presented as a series of *cūttiram*s (Sanskrit *sūtra*), or brief verse-sayings. The *Tolkāppiyam* has 1,612 *cūttiram*s. There are at least seven commentaries, preserved in part or in their entirety; the earliest is Iḷampūraṇar (eleventh-twelfth century), and the most recent is a seventeenth-century anonymous one (See: A.K. Ramanujan 1985:302).

25. Of the seven types, only the middle five are the subject of true love poetry. The hero and heroine should be "well-matched in ten points" such as beauty, wealth, age, virtue, rank, etc. Only such as pair is capable of the full range of love: union and separation, anxiety, patience, betrayal, forgiveness. The couple must be cultured; for the uncultured will be rash, ignorant, self-centered, and therefore unfit for *akam* poetry (See: A.K. Ramanujan 1985:236).

26. *māveṉa maḍalum ūrba pūveṉak*
    kuvimugiḻ erukkam kaṇṇiyum cūḍuba
    maṟugiṉ ārkkavum paḍuba
    piṟidum āguba kāmamkāḻ koḻiṉē
    (Pēreyiṉ Muṟuvalār, *Kuṟuntogai* 17)

27. *miṉṉoḻir aviraṟal iḍaipōḻum peyalēpōl*
     poṉṉagai tagaivagir vagaineṟi vayaṅgiṭṭup
     pōḻiḍai iṭṭa kamaḻnaṟum pūṅkōdai
     iṉṉagai ilaṅgeyiṟṟut tēmoḻittuvarc cevvāy
     nalnudāl niṉakkoṉṟu kūṟuvām kēḻiṉi
     nilleṉa niṟuttāṉ niṟuttē vandu
     nudalum mugaṉum tōḻum kaṇṇum
     iyalum collum nōkkubu niṉai-i
     aitēyn daṉṟu piṟaiyum aṉṟu
     maitīrn daṉṟu madiyum aṉṟu
     vēyamaṉ raṉṟu malaiyum aṉṟu
     pūvamaṉ raṉṟu cuṉaiyum aṉṟu
     mella iyalum mayilum aṉṟu
     collat taḻarum kiḻiyum aṉṟu
     eṉavāṅgu
     aṉaiyaṉa palapā rāṭṭip paiyeṉa
     valaivar pōlac cōrpadaṉ oṟṟip
     pulaiyar pōlap pūṅkaṉ nōkkit
     toḻalum toḻudāṉ toḍalum toṭṭāṉ
     kalvarai nillāk kaḍuṅkaḻi raṉṉōṉ
     toḻū-um toḍū-umavaṉ taṉmai
     ēḻait taṉmaiyō illai tōḻi
     (Kabilar, *Kalittogai* 55)

28. *kālaiyum pagalum kaiyaṟu mālaiyum*
     ūrtuñcu yāmamum viḍiyalum eṉṟip
     poḻudiḍai teriyiṉ poyyē kāmam
     māveṉa maḍaloḍu maṟugil tōṉṟit
     teṟṟeṉat tūṟṟalum paḻiyē
     vāḻdalum paḻiyē pirivutalai variṉē.
     (Aḷḷūr Naṉmullaiyār, *Kuṟuntogai* 32)

29. http://Sangamtranslationsbyvaidehi.wordpress.com/kurunthokai-1-
     100/

30. *eṉ nōṟ raṉaikollō!*
     nīruḷ niḻalpōl nuḍaṅgiya meṉcāyal
     īṅguruc curuṅgi
     iyaluvāy niṉṉō ḍucāvuvēṉ niṉṟīttai
     aṉṉaiyō kāṇtagaiyillāk kuṟaḷnālip pōḻdiṉāṉ
     āṇtalaik kīṉra paraḻmagaṉē nīyemmai
     vēṇḍuva leṉṟu vilakkiṉai niṉpōlvār
     tīṇḍap perubavō maṟṟu

māṇḍa eṛitta paḍaipōl muḍaṅgi maḍaṅgi
neṛittuviṭ ṭaṉṉa niṛaiērāl eṉṉaip
poṛukkallā nōyceydāy poṛī-i niṛukkallēṉ
nīnalgiṉ uṇḍeṉ uyir
kuṛippukkāṉ valluppalagai eḍuttu niṛuttaṉṉa
kallāk kuṛaḷa kaḍumpagal vandemmai
illattu vāveṉa meykoḷī-i ellāniṉ
peṇḍir uḷarmaṉṉō kūṛu
nallāykēḷ ukkattu mēlum naḍuvuyarndu vālvāya
kokkurit taṉṉa koḍumaḍāy niṉṉaiyāṉ
pukkagalam pulliṉeñ cūṉrum puṛampulliṉ
akkuḷuttup pullalum āṛṛēṉ aruḷīmō
pakkattup pullac ciṛidu
pōcīttai makkaḷ muriyēnī māṛiṉīt tokka
marakkōṭṭañ cērndeḷunda pūṅkoḍi pōla
nirappamil yākkai taḷī-iyiṉar emmaip
purappēm eṉbārum palarāṛ parattaiyeṉ
pakkattup pullīyā yeṉṉumāl tokka
uḷundiṉum tuvvāk kuṛuvaṭṭā niṉṉiṉ
iḷindadō kūṉiṉ piṛappu kaḷindāṅgē
yāmvīḷdum eṉrutaṉ piṉcelavu muṛṛiyāk
kūṉi kuḷaiyum kuḷaivukāṉ
yāmai eḍuttu niṛuttaṛṛāl tōḷiraṇḍum vīci
yāmvēṇḍē meṉru vilakkavum emvīḷum
kāmar naḍakkum naḍaikāṉ kavarkaṇaic
cāmaṉār tammuṉ celavukāṉ
ō-okāṉ nammuḷ nakudaṛ toḍī-iyar nammuḷnām
ucāvavum kōṉaditoṭ ṭēṉ
āṅgāga cāyaliṉ mārba aḍaṅkiṉēṉ ēe
pēyum pēyum tuḷḷal uṛumeṉak
kōyiluṭ kaṇḍār nagāmai vēṇḍuval
taṇḍāt tagaḍuruva vēṛāgak kāviṉkīḷp
pōda rakaḍārap pulli muyaṅguvēm
tugaḷtabu kāṭci avaiyattār ōlai

mugaḍukāppu yāttuviṭ ṭāṅgu

(Marudaṉiḷa Nāgaṉār, *Kalittogai* 94)

31. *tirundiḷāy keḷāy nammūrk kellām cālum*
    perunagai algal nigaḷnda torunilaiyē
    maṉpadai ellām maḍinda iruṅkaṅgul
    antugil pōrvai aṇipeṛa tai-inam
    iṉcāyal mārbaṉ kuṛiniṉrēṉ yāṉāgat

tīrat taṟainda talaiyuntaṉ kambalum
kārak kuṟaindu kaṟaippaṭṭu vandunam
cēriyiṟ pōgā muḍamudir pārppāṉait
tōḻinī pōṟṟudi eṉṟi yavaṉāṅgē
pārāk kuḻaṟāp paṇiyāp poḻudaṉṟi
yārivaṉ niṉṟīr eṉakkūṟip paiyeṉa
vaikāṉ muḍupagaṭṭiṟ pakkattiṟ pōgādu
taiyāl tambalam tiṉṟiyō eṉrutaṉ
pakkaḻittuk koṇḍī eṉattaraulm yādoṉṟum
vāyvāḷēṉ niṟpak kaḍidagaṉṟu kaimāṟik
kaippaḍukkap paṭṭāy ciṟuminī maṟṟiyāṉ
ēṉai picācaruḷ eṉṉai nalitariṉ
ivvūrp palinī peṟāmaṟ koḷvēṉ
eṉappalavum tāṅgādu vāypāḍi niṟpa
muḍupārppāṉ añciṉaṉādal aṟindiyāṉ eñcādu
orukai maṉarkoṇḍu mēṟṟūvak kaṇḍē
kaḍida raṟrip pūcal toḍaṅgiṉa ṉāṅgē
oḍuṅgā vayattiṟ koḍuṅkēḻk kaḍuṅkaṇ
irumpuli koṇmār niṟutta valaiyuḷōr
ēdil kuṟunari paṭṭaṟṟāṟ kādalaṉ
kāṭci aḻuṅga nammūrk kelā-am
āgula māgi viḷaindadai eṉrumtaṉ
vāḻkkai aduvāgak koṇḍa muḍupārppāṉ
vīḻkkaip peruṅkarum kūttu
(Kabilar, *Kalittogai* 65)

32. *nīrniṟam karappa vūḻuṟu budirndu*
    pūmalar kañaliya kaḍuvaraṟ kāṉyāṟṟu
    karā-am tuñcum kalluyar maṟiculi
    marā-a yāṉai madamtaba oṟri
    urā-a vīrkkum uṭkuvaru nīttam
    kaḍuṅkaṇ paṉṟiyiṉ naḍuṅkādu tuṇindu
    nāma varunturaip pērtandu yāmattu
    īṅgum varubavō ōṅgal veṟpa
    orunāḷ viḻumam uṟiṉum vaḻināḷ
    vāḻguvaḷ allaḷ eṉtōḻi yāvadum
    ūril vaḻigaḷum payila vaḻaṅgunar
    nīḍiṉṟāga iḻukkuvar adaṉāl
    ulamaral varutta muṟudumem paḍappaik
    koḍuntēṉ iḻaitta kōḍuyar neḍuvaraip
    paḻantūṅgu naḷippiṟ kāntaḷam podumbil
    pagalnī variṉum puṇarguvai agaṉmalai

vāṅgamaik kaṇṇiḍai kaḍuppa yāy
ōmbiṉaḷ eḍutta taḍameṉ tōḷē
(Kabilar, *Akanāṉūṟu* 18)

33. Source: http://Sangamtranslationsbyvaidehi.com/akananuru-1-50/

34. *māmalar muṇḍagam tillaiyōḍu oruṅguḍaṉ*
     kāṉal aṇinda uyarmaṉal ekkarmēl
     cīrmigu ciṟappiṉōṉ maramudaṟ kaicērtta
     nīrmali karagampōl paḻantūṅgu muḍattāḻaip
     pūmalarn davaipōlap puḷḷalgum tuṟaivakēḷ
     āṟṟuda leṉbadoṉ ṟalandavark kudavudal
     pōṟṟuda leṉbadu puṇardāraip piriyāmai
     paṉbeṉap paḍuvadu pāḍaṟin doḻugudal
     aṉbeṉap paḍuvadu taṉkiḷai cerāmai
     ariveṉap paḍuvadu pēdaiyārcol nōṉṟal
     ceriveṉap paḍuvadu kūṟiyadu maṟāmai
     niṟaiyeṉap paḍuvadu maṟaipiṟar aṟiyāmai
     muṟaiyenap paḍuvadu kaṇṇōḍā duyirvauval
     poṟaiyeṉap paḍuvadu pōṟṟāraip poṟuttal
     āṅgadai aṟindaṉi rāyiṉeṉ tōḷi
     naṉṉudal nalaṉuṇḍu tuṟattal koṉga
     tīmpāl uṇbavar koḷkalam varaidal
     ceṉṟaṉai kaḷaimō pūṉganiṉ tērē
     (Nallanduvaṉār, *Kalittogai* 133)

35. Source: http://Sangamtranslationsbyvaidehi.com/a-kalithokai-
     neythal/

36. *amma vāḻi tōḻi kādalar*
     nilampuḍai peyarva dāyiṉum kūṟiya
     coṟpuḍai peyardalō ilarē vāṉam
     naḷikaḍal mugandu ceṟitaga iruḷik
     kaṉaipeyal poḻindu kaḍuṅkural payiṟṟi
     kārcey teṉṉuḷai yaduvē āyiḍaik
     kollaik kōvalar elli māṭṭiya
     perumara oḍiyal pōla
     aruḷilēṉ amma aḷiyēṉ yāṉē.
     (Maruṅgūrp Paṭṭiṉattuc Cēndaṉ Kumaraṉār, *Naṟṟiṇai* 289)

37. Source: http://Sangamtranslationsbyvaidehi.com/natrinai-201-300/

38. *āḍamai puraiyum vaṉappiṉ paṇaittōḷ*
    pēramark kaṇṇi irunda ūrē
    neḍuñcēṉ āriḍai yaduvē neñcē
    īram paṭṭa cevvip paimpuṉattu
    ōrēr uḻavaṉ pōlap
    peruvidup puṟṟaṉṟāl nōgō yāṉē
    (Ōrēruḻavaṉār, *Kuṟuntogai*, 131)

39. *niṉṉē pōlum maññai yālaniṉ*
    naṉṉudal nāṟum mullai malara
    niṉṉē pōla māmaruṇḍu nōkka
    niṉṉē uḷḷi vandaṉeṉ
    naṉṉudal arivai kāriṉum viraindē
    (Pēyaṉār, *Aiṅkuṟunūṟu* 492)

40. *vāṉam vāyppak kaviṉik kāṉam*
    kamañcul māmalai kāṟpayan diṟutteṉa
    maṇimaruḷ pūvai yaṇimala riḍai-iḍaic
    cempuṟa mūdāy parattaliṉ, naṉpala
    mullai vīkaḻal tā-ay vallōṉ
    ceygai aṉṉa cennilap puṟaviṉ
    vā-ap pāṇi vayaṅgutoḻiṟ kalimāt
    tā-at tāḻiṉai mella oduṅga,
    iḍimaraṉ dēmadi vaḻava! kuvimugai
    vāḻai vāṉpū vūḻuṟu budirnda
    oḻikulai yaṉṉa tirimarup pēṟṟoḍu
    kaṇaikkā lampiṇaik kāmar puṇarnilai
    kaḍumāṉ tēroli kēṭpiṉ
    naḍunāḷ kūṭṭam āgalum uṇḍē
    (Cīttalai Cāttaṉār, *Akanāṉūṟu* 134).

41. *cēṟṟunilai muṉai-iya ceṅkaṭ kārāṉ*
    ūrmaḍi kaṅgulil nōṉṭalai parindu
    kūrmuḷ vēli kōṭṭi ṉīkki
    nīrmudir paḻanattu mīṉuḍa ṉiriya
    antūmbu vaḷḷai mayakkit tāmarai
    vaṇḍūdu paṇimala rāru mūra
    yārai yōniṟ pulakkēm, vāruṟṟu
    uṟai-iṟandu, oḻirum tāḻirum kūndaṟ
    piṟaru moruttiyai nammaṉait tandu
    vaduvai yayarndaṉai eṉba ahdiyām
    kūṟēm vāḻiya rendai ceṟunar
    kaḻiṟuḍai yaruñcamam tadaiya nūṟum

oḷiruvāṭ ṭāṉaik koṟṟac ceḻiyaṉ
piṇḍa nelliṉ Aḷḷūr aṉṉayeṉ
oṇṭoḍi ñegiḻiṉum ñegiḻga;
ceṉṟī perumaniṟ ṟagaikkunar yārō?
(Aḷḷūr Naṉmullaiyār, *Akanāṉūṟu* 46)

42. Source: http://Sangamtranslationsbyvaidehi.com/akananuru-1-50/

43. *muḷḷeyiṟṟup pāṇmaga ḷiṉkeḍiṟu corinda*
     agaṉperu vaṭṭi niṟaiya maṉaiyōḷ
     arikāṟ perumpayaṟu niṟaikku mūra
     māṇiḻai āya maṟiyuniṉ
     pāṇaṉ pōlap palapoyt tallē.
     (Ōrampōgiyār, *Aiṅkuṟunūṟu* 47)

     valaival pāṇmagaṉ vāleyiṟṟup maḍamagaḷ
     varā-al corinda vaṭṭiyuṉ maṉaiyōḷ
     yāṇḍukaḻi veṇṇel niṟaikku mūra
     veṇḍēm perumaniṉ parattai
     āṇḍuccey kuṟiyō ḍiṇḍunī varalē.
     (Ōrampōgiyār, *Aiṅkuṟunūṟu* 48)

44. Source:http://Sangamtranslationsbyvaidehi.wordpress.com/ainkuru-
     nuru-marutham-orampokiyar-1-100/

45. Source:http://Sangamtranslationsbyvaidehi.wordpress.com/ainkuru-
     nuru-marutham-orampokiyar-1-100/

46. *guṇakaḍaṟ ṟiraiyadu paṟaitabu nārai*
     tiṇtērp poṟaiyaṉ toṇḍi muṉṟuṟai
     ayirai yāriraik kaṇavan dā-aṅguc
     cēyaḷ ariyōḷ paḍardi
     nōyai neñcē nōyppā lōyē.
     (Paraṇar, *Kuṟuntogai*, 128)

     maṉṉuyi raṟiyāt tuṉṉarum potiyiṟ
     cūruḍai yaḍukkat tāraṅ kaḍuppa
     vēṇi lāṉē taṉṉiyaḷ paṇiyē
     vāṅgukadir toguppak kūmbi yaiyeṉa
     alaṅguveyiṟ podinda tāmarai
     uḷḷagat taṉṉa ciṟuvem maiyaḷē
     (Paḍumarattu Mōcikoṟṟṉār, *Kuṟuntogai*, 376)

47. Source:http://Sangamtranslationsbyvaidehi.wordpress.com/kurun-thokai-101-200/

48. Source:http://Sangamtranslationsbyvaidehi.wordpress.com/kurun-thokai-301-400/

49. *nōmeṉ neñcē nōmeṉ neñcē*
    imaitīyp paṉṉa kaṇṇīr tāṅgi
    amaidaṟ kamaindanaṅ kādalar
    amaivila rāgudal nōmeṉ neñcē.
    (Kāmañcēr Kuḷattār, *Kuṟuntogai* 4)

50. Source: http://Sangamtranslationsbyvaidehi.wordpress.com/kurun-thokai- 1-100/

51. *kaḍumpuṉal toḍutta naḍuṅgañar aḷḷaṟ*
    kavirida ḻaṉṉa tūvic cevvāy
    iraitēr nāraikku evva māgat
    tū-un tuvalait tuyarkūr vāḍaiyum
    vārār pōlvarnam kādalar
    vālēṉ pōlval tōḻi yāṉē.
    (Vāyilāṉ Dēvaṉār, *Kuṟuntogai* 103)

52. Source: http://Sangamtranslationsbyvaidehi.wordpress.com/kurun-thokai-101-200/

53. *ceṉru nīḍuṉa rallar avarvayiṉ*
    iṉaidal āṉāy eṉriciṉ iguḷai
    ambutoḍai yamaidi kāṇmār vambalar
    kalaṉila rāyiṉum koṉrupuḷ ḷūṭṭum
    kallā iḷaiyar kalitta kavalaik
    kaṇaṉari iṉaṉoḍu kuḻī-i niṇaṉarundum
    neyttō rāḍiya mallaṉ mociviral
    atta eruvaic cēval cērnda
    araicēr yātta veṇtiraḷ viṉaiviṟal
    eḻā-at tiṇitōḷ cōḻar perumagaṉ
    viḷaṅgupugaḻ nirutta iḷamperuṅ ceṉṉi
    kuḍikkaḍa ṉāgaliṟ kuṟaiviṉai muḍimār
    cempuṟaḷ puricaip pāḻi nūṟi
    vamba vaḍugar paintalai cavaṭṭik
    koṉra yāṉaik kōṭṭiṟ ṟōṉrum
    añcuvaru marabiṉ veñcura miṟandōr

nōyilar peyarda laṟiyiṉ
āḻala maṉṉō tōḻiyeṉ kaṇṇē.
(Iḍaiyaṉ Cēndaṅkoṟṟaṉār, *Akanāṉūṟu* 375)

54. *arumporuḷ vēṭkaiyiṉ uḷḷam turappap*
     pirintuṟai cūlādi yaiya virumpinī
     eṉtō ḷeḷudiya toyyilum yāḻaniṉ
     maintuḍai mārbil cuṇaṅgum niṉaittukkāṇ
     ceṉṟōr mugappap poruḷum kiḍavādu
     oḻindava rellāru muṇṇāduñ cellār
     Iḷamaiyuṅ kāmamu mōrāṅgup peṟṟār
     vaḷamai viḷaitakka duṇḍo uḷanāḷ
     ōrō-ogai tammuḷ taḻī-i yōrō-ogai
     oṉṟaṉkū ṟāḍai uḍuppavarē yāyiṉum
     oṉṟiṉār vāḻkkaiyē vāḻkkai yaritarō
     ceṉṟa iḷamai taraṟku.
     (Pālai Pāḍiya Peruṅkaḍuṅkō, *Kalittogai* 18)

55. Source: http://Sangamtranslationsbyvaidehi.com/kalithokai-palai/

56. *kuṟuntāḷ kūdaḷi yāḍiya neḍuvaraip*
     peruntēṉ kaṇḍa iruṅga(ī)ṉ muḍavaṉ
     uṭkaic ciṟukuḍai kōlik kīḻirindu
     cuṭṭubu nakki yāṅguk kādalar
     nalgār nayavār āyiṉum
     palkāl kāṇḍalum uḷḷattuk kiṉidē
     (Paraṇar, *Kuṟuntogai* 60)

57. Source: http://Sangamtranslationsbyvaidehi.wordpress.com/kurun-
     thokai-1-100/

58. *aruḷum aṉbum nīkkit tuṇaituṟandu*
     poruḷvayiṟ pirivō ruravō rāyiṉ
     uravō ruravō rāga
     maḍava māga maḍandai nāmē.
     (Kōpperuñcōḻaṉ, *Kuṟuntogai* 20)

59. *melliyal arivainiṉ nallagam pulamba*
     niṟṟuṟandu amaiguve ṉāyiṉ eṟṟuṟandu
     iravalar vārā vaigal
     palavā gugayāṉ celavuṟu tagavē
     (Pālai Pāḍiya Peruṅkaḍuṅkō, *Kuṟuntogai* 137)

60. Source: http://Sangamtranslationsbyvaidehi.wordpress.com/kurun-
    thokai-101-200/

61. *vīṅguvicaip piṇitta viraipari neḍuntēr*
    nōṉkadir cumanda āḻiyāḻ maruṅgir
    pāmbeṉa muḍugunī rōḍak kūmbip
    parruviḍu viraliṟ payaṟukā yūḻppa
    arciram niṉraṉrāṟ poḻudē muṟpaḍa
    āḷviṉaik keḻunda acaivi luḷḷattu
    āṇmai vāṅgak kāmam taṭpak
    kavaipaḍu neñcam kaṭka ṉagaiya
    irutalaik koḷḷi iḍainiṉru varundi
    orutalaip paḍā-a uṟavi pōṉraṉam
    nōṅkol aḷiyaḷ tāṉē yākkaikku
    uyiriyain daṉṉa naṭpi ṉavvuyir
    vāḻda laṉṉa kādal
    cāda laṉṉa pirivari yōḷē
    (Naraimuḍi Neṭṭaiyār, *Akanāṉūṟu* 339)

    puṟantāḻ biruṇḍa kūndaṟ pōdiṉ
    nirampeṟu mīridalp polinda vuṇkaṇ
    uḷḷam piṇikkoṉ ḍōḷvayiṉ neñcam
    cellal tīrgam celvā meṉṉum
    ceyviṉai muḍiyā devvam ceydal
    eyyā maiyō ḍiḷivutalait tarumeṉa
    uṟudi tūkkat tūṅgi aṟivē
    ciṟiduṉaṉi viraiya leṉṉum āyiḍai
    oḷiṟēndu maruppiṟ kaḷiṟumāṟu paṟriya
    tēypurip paḻaṅkayiṟu pōla
    vīvadu kolleṉ varundiya vuḍambē.
    (Tēypurip Paḻaṅkayiṟṟṉār, *Naṟriṇai* 284)

62. Source: http://Sangamtranslationsbyvaidehi.com/akananuru-301-
    400/

63. Source: http://Sangamtranslationsbyvaidehi.com/natrinai-201-300/

64. *īdaluṉ tuyttalum illōrkku illeṉac*
    ceyviṉai kaimmiga eṉṉudi avviṉaikku
    ammā varivaiyum varumō
    emmai yuyttiyō uraitticiṉ neñcē
    (Ugāykkuḍi Kiḻār, *Kuṟuntogai* 63)

65. Source: http://Sangamtranslationsbyvaidehi.wordpress.com/kurun-thokai-1-100/

66. *marundeṉiṉ marundē vaippeṉiṉ vaippē*
 arumbiya cuṇaṅgiṉ ampakaṭṭu iḷamulaip
 peruntōḷ nuṇugiya nucuppiṉ
 kalkeḻu kāṉavar nalkuṟu magaḷē
 (Karuvūr Ōdañāṉiyār, *Kuṟuntogai* 71)

67. Source: http://Sangamtranslationsbyvaidehi.wordpress.com/kurun-thokai-1-100/

68. *aṇṇāṉ dēndiya vaṉamulai taḷariṉum*
 poṉṉēr mēṉi maṇiyiṉ tāḻnda
 naṉṉeḍuṅ kūndal naraiyoḍu muḍippiṉum
 nīttal ōmbumadi pukkē ḻūra
 iṉkaḍuṅ kaḷḷiṉ iḷaiyaṇi neḍuntērk
 koṟṟac cōḻar koṅgarp paṇī-iyar
 veṇkōṭṭu yāṉaip pō-or kiḻavōṉ
 paḻaiyaṉ vēlvāyt taṉṉaniṉ
 piḷaiyā naṉmoḻi tēṟiya ivaṭkē.
 (Unknown Poet, *Naṟṟiṇai* 10)

69. Source: http://Sangamtranslationsbyvaidehi.com/natrinai-1-100/

70. *koḍuṅtāḷ mudalaik kōḷval ēṟṟai*
 vaḻivaḻak karukkum kāṉalam peruntuṟai
 iṉamīṉ iruṅkaḻi nīndi nīniṉ
 nayaṉuḍai maiyiṉ varudi ivaḷtaṉ
 maḍaṉuḍai maiyiṉ uyaṅgum yāṉadu
 kavaimaga nañcuṇ ḍāṅgu
 añcuval peruma eṉṉeñcat tāṉē.
 (Kavai Magaṉār, *Kuṟuntogai* 324)

71. Source: http://Sangamtranslationsbyvaidehi.wordpress.com/kurun-thokai-301-400/

72. *nīyēpuṟavi nalla laṉṟiyum piṟavum*
 iḍukkaṇ palavum viḍuttōṉ maruganai
 ivarēpulaṉuḻu duṇmār puṉka ṇañcit
 tamadupagut tuṇṇum taṉṉilal vāḻnar
 kaḷirukaṇ ḍalū-um aḻā-al maṟanda
 puṉtalaic ciṟā-ar maṉṟumaruṇḍu nōkki

virundir puṇkaṇō vuḍaiyar
kēṭṭaṇai yāyiṇī vēṭṭadu ceymmē.
(Kōvūr Kiḻār, *Purananuru* 46)

73. *irumpaṇai veṇtōḍu malaindō ṇallaṇ*
karuñciṇai vēmbiṇ teriyalō ṇallaṇ
niṇṇa kaṇṇiyu mārmiḍain daṇrē niṇṇnoḍu
poruvōṇ kaṇṇiyu mārmiḍain daṇrē
oruvīr tōrpiṇum tōrpanum kuḍiyē
iruvīr vēra liyarkaiyu maṇrē adaṇāl
kuḍipporu ḷaṇrunum ceydi koḍittēr
nummō raṇṇa vēndarkku
meymmali yuvagai ceyyumiv vigalē.
(Kōvūr Kiḻār to Neḍuṅkiḷḷi and Nalaṅkiḷḷi, *Puranāṇūru* 45)

74. *irumpiḍit toḻudiyoḍu peruṅkayam paḍiyā*
nelluḍaik kavaḷamoṭu neymmidi perā-a
tirundarai nōṇveḷil varunda vorri
nilamicaip puraḷum kaiya veyduyirttu
alamaral yāṇai yurumeṇa muḻaṅgavum
pālil kuḻavi alaravum magaḷir
pūvil varuntalai muḍippavum nīril
viṇaipuṇai nallil iṇaikū-uk kēṭpavum
iṇṇādu amma īṅgiṇi diruttal
tuṇṇarun tuppiṇ vayamāṇ tōṇral
aravai yāyi ṇiṇadeṇat tirattal
maravai yāyir pōroḍu tirattal
aravaiyu maravaiyu mallai yāgat
tiravā daḍaitta tiṇṇilaik kadaviṇ
nīḷmadil orucirai yoḍuṅgudal
nāṇuttaga vuḍaittidu kāṇuṅ kālē.
(Kōvūr Kiḻār to Neḍuṅkiḷḷi, *Puranāṇūru* 44)

75. Source: http://Sangamtranslationsbyvaidehi.com/purananuru-1-50/

76. Pēgaṇ was one of the seven great donors, who were small-region kings. The seven are Kāri, Ōri, Pēgaṇ, Āy, Nalli, Pāri and Atigaṇ – Atigaṇ is Atiyamāṇ, who is mentioned as Eḻiṇi (his clan name).

77. *kuḻavi yirappiṇum ūṇtaḍi pirappiṇum*
āḷaṇ reṇru vāḷir rappār
toḍarppaḍu ñamaliyiṇ iḍarppaḍut tirī-iya
kēḷal kēḷir vēḷāṇ cirupadam

madukai yiṉṟi vayiṟṟuttī taṇiyat
tāmiran duṇṇu maḷavai
īṉma rōviv vulagat tāṉē
(Cēramāṉ Kaṇaikkāl Irumpoṟai, *Puranāṉūṟu* 74)

78. Source: http://Sangamtranslationsbyvaidehi.com/purananuru-51-100

79. Pulkit Sharma, "We Need To Rehabilitate The 'Dark' Mind," *Speaking Tree*, The Times of India, Delhi Edition, 16th Jan. 2015, p. 24.

80. It is obvious that during the course of our daily life, we swing into various moods in response to stimuli from sense objects. We also react to people, places, and situations resulting in a constant change in our behavior pattern. Hindu scriptures attribute these changes to inborn qualities called *guṇas*, which are classified as *satva* (purity), *rajas* (passion), and *tamas* (dullness).

Bhagavad Gita and *Bhagavatham* enlighten us on these *guṇas*. Our various activities always exhibit these *guṇas* that constantly overlap forcing us to swing into various moods and behavior. When we pray, meditate, or listen to music we are *satvik* (pure). When we attend to our household or office work, we are *rajasik* (active). When we are lazy and lie down quietly we are *tamasik* (dull).

Bhagavad Gita explains: "*Satva* prevails overlapping *rajas* and *tamas*; *rajas* prevails overlapping *satva* and *tamas*; *tamas* manifests itself overlapping *satva* and *rajas*."

In the *Bhagavatam*, Krishna tells his friend Uddhava: "There is predominance of one or the other *guṇas* in things, objects and persons. Our deeds and thoughts always express one *guna* or the other. Indeed, every object in this manifold universe and even celestial beings are influenced by these *guṇas*."

Bhagavad Gita: *Mokshe Sanyasa Yoga* confirms this: "There is no being, animate or inanimate, on earth or in the middle region or even among gods and devas or anywhere else, which is free from these three *guṇas* born of nature."

Guṇas influence everything in creation. Let us see a few examples:
Sky: Puffy clouds are *satvik*; thunder and lightning are *rajasik*; and
      a clear sky is *tamasik*.

Wind: A mild breeze is *satvik*, a cyclone is *rajasik*, and still weather
  is *tamasik*.
Water: A fountain in the park is *satvik*; waterfall is *rajasik*; and
  a lake is *tamasik*.
Fire: Candlelight is *satvik*; a raging fire is *rajasik*, and smoldering
  fire is *tamasik*.
Animal: A lion playing with cubs is *satvik*; chasing its prey is *rajasik*; and resting under the shade is *tamasik*.
Bird: A nesting bird is *satvik*; flying around to pick worms is *rajasik*; and resting on a branch is *tamasik*.
Insect: A busy caterpillar is *rajasik*; the cocoon is *tamasik*; and the
  butterfly is *satvik*.

The Bhagavad Gita explains how these *guṇas* manifest in us:
Satva: Being immaculate is illuminating and flawless and leads to
  joy and wisdom.
Rajas: Passion results in longing and attachment, motivating the
  individual to action and to face the consequences.
Tamas: Ignorance deludes through negligence, inactivity, laziness,
  and sleep.

In the *Bhagavatam*, Krishna tells Uddhava, "When *satva*, which is
pure and tranquil and has the power to illumine, overcomes *rajas*
and *tamas,* the person is endowed with happiness, virtue and
knowledge. "When *rajas*, which leads the person to action and results in attachment ensuing the vision of multiplicity, overcomes
satva and *tamas*, the person is active, finds wealth, fame, and suffers misery. "When *tamas*, which is characterized by inertia and
casts a veil of ignorance on one's mind and makes the person, lose
the power of discrimination, overcomes *satva* and *rajas* the person
is stricken with grief and delusion. He lives in a dream of hope and,
to fulfill the same, he even becomes cruel. Laziness and inertia sets
in."

The *Bhagavad Gita* confirms this: "Those who are settled in *satva*
go upward, *rajasiks* dwell in the middle, and *tamasiks* remaining
under the influence of the lowest qualities go downward."

Krishna tells Uddhava: "These three *guṇas* belong to the mind and
not to yourself. Rise above the *guṇas* and realize the self. First
overcome *rajas* and *tamas* by developing *satva* and then rise above
satva by *satva* itself."

Become a *satvik* to realize you are the higher self-caged in the lower self-comprising of the body-mind-intellect complex. To be a *satvik* you need not be docile, obedient, lose interest in life or give up your choice food, recreation, and hobbies and sit in meditation for long hours! What you have to do is to spend some time every day in solitude, silence and contemplation. The best time to do this is just before retiring at night. Sit in contemplation for 15 minutes identifying yourself one with your *ishta deivam* (favorite god) ever present in your heart.

As these *guṇas* constantly overlap your daily life, get into a *satvik* mood as often as possible. The mind manifests these *guṇas* based on the stimuli received from sense objects, situations and circumstances. Be a *satvik* by controlling your mind and relinquish all actions to your lower self. Look within yourself to be a *satvik* and you will radiate peace, tranquility, joy and happiness forever.
(Source: https://www.indiacurrents.com/articles/2011/12/14/three-guṇas)

In the *Bhagavad Gita* (the Seventeenth chapter - *Shrada Treta Yog*), Lord Krishna tells about the three kinds of faith, the three kinds of penance and austerity, and the three attributes of nature. While explaining about the three *guṇas* of human beings, Lord Krishna explains that nature, *maya* or illusion has three qualities – *satva*, *rajas* and *tamas*. The thoughts that we think, the pleasures that we get here, the service that we render – everything has this three-fold division. The man who wishes to develop divine qualities always chooses the *satvik* in everything. He eats *satvik* food, performs *satvik* worship and satvik thoughts. The *satvik* people worship the different forms of God, the *rajasik* worship the gods of power and wealth, while the *tamasik* worship spirits and ghosts. The person who does not expect any reward, appreciation is *satvik*. *Rajasik* is a person who expects a return or reward. *Tamasik* is the person who does charity to the undeserved at the wrong time and place. People who love ostentation and showing off, who are full of arrogance and lust, who perform severe austerities motivated only by the desires to acquire things, are of demonic nature.
(Source: http://www.speakingtree.in/spiritual-slideshow/seekers/
philosophy/who-is-satvik-rajasik-tamasik- person/84876)

81. Anup Taneja, 'When The Mind Becomes A Battlefield', *The Speaking Tree*, Times of India, Delhi Edition, Dated 13th November 2014, P. 16.

82. *muṭṭu vēṉkol tākku vēṉkol*
    ōrēṉ yāṉumōr peṟṟi mēliṭṭu
    āa olleṉak kūvu vēṉkol
    alamara lacaivaḷi yalaippaveṉ
    uyavunō yaṟiyādu tuñcu mūrkkē.
    (Avvaiyār, *Kuṟuntogai* 28)

83. Source: http://Sangamtranslationsbyvaidehi.wordpress.com/kurun-thokai-1-100/

84. "The term, 'hysteria' is derived from the Greek word *hustera*, meaning 'womb' or 'uterus' as it was believed in the distant past that the symptoms with which women presented, for which no obvious cause could be detected, originated from malfunctioning of the womb. The term mass hysteria is applied to situations in which a large group of people exhibit the same kinds of physical symptoms with no organic cause" (See: Sunil K. Pandya 2013:161).

85. *maḷḷar kuḻī-iya viḻavi ṉāṉum*
    magaḷir taḻī-iya tuṇaṅgai yāṉum
    yāṇdum kāṉēṉ māṉtak kōṉai
    yāṉum ōrāḍukaḷa magaḷē yeṉkaik
    kōḍī rilaṅguvaḷai ñegiḻtta
    pīḍukeḻu kuricilumō rāḍukaḷa magaṉē.
    (Ādimandi, *Kuṟuntogai* 31)

86. Source: http://Sangamtranslationsbyvaidehi.wordpress.com/kurun-thokai-1-100/

87. *kaḍuntēr kuḻitta ñeḷḷa lāṅkaṉ*
    veḷvāyk kaḻudaip pulliṉam pūṭṭip
    pāḻcey taṉaiyavar naṉantalai nalleyil
    puḷḷiṉam imiḻum pugaḻcāl viḷaivayal
    veḷḷuḷaik kalimāṉ kavikuḷam bugala
    tērvaḷaṅ kiṉainiṉ tevvar tē-ettut
    tuḷaṅgiyalāṟ paṇaiyeruttiṟ
    pā-aḍiyāṟ ceṟanōkkiṉ
    oḷirumaruppiṟ kaḷiṟavara
    kāppuḍaiya kayampaḍiyiṉai
    aṉṉa cīṟṟat taṉaiyai yāgaliṉ
    viḷaṅgupoṉ ṉeṟinda nalaṅkiḷar palakaiyoḍu
    niḻalpaḍu neḍuvē lēndi yoṉṉār
    oṇpaḍaik kaḍuntār muṉbutalaik koṇmār

nacaitara vandōr nacaipirak koḷiya
vacaipaṭa vāḷndōr palarkol puraiyil
narpanuval nālvēdattu
aruñcīrttip peruṅkaṇṇurai
neymmali y āvudi poṅgap paṉmāṇ
vīyāc cirappiṉ vēḷvi murri
yūba naṭṭa viyaṉkaḷam palakol
yāpala kollō peruma vārurru
vicipiṇik koṇḍa maṇkaṉai muḷaviṟ
pāḍiṉi pāḍum vañcikku
nāḍal cāṉra maindinōy niṉakkē.
(Neṭṭimaiyār to Pāṇḍiyaṉ Palyāgacālai Mudukuḍumip Peruvaḷudi,
  Purananūru 15)

88. Source: http://Sangamtranslationsbyvaidehi.com/purananuru-1-50/

89. *nudivēl koṇḍu nudalviyar tuḍaiyāk*
     kaḍiya kūrum vēndē tandaiyum
     neḍiya valladu paṇindu moḷiyaḷaṉē
     ihdivar paḍiva māyin vaiyeyirru
     arimadar maḷaikkaṇ ammā varivai
     marampaḍu cirutīp pōla
     aṇaṅgā yiṉaḷtāṉ piranda vūrkkē
     (Madurai Marudaṇiḷa Nāgaṉār, *Purananūru* 349)

90. Source: http://Sangamtranslationsbyvaidehi.com/purananuru-301-
     350/

References

Tamil̲ Sources (Primary)

Akanāṉūr̲u, 1966, Edited with a commentary by P.V. Somasundaranar, Chennai: South India Saiva Siddhanta Works Publishing Society.

Aiṅkur̲unūr̲u, 1979, Edited with a commentary by P.V. Somasundaranar, Chennai: South India Saiva Siddhanta Works Publishing Society.

Kalittogai, 1981 (Rpt.), With a commentary by Naccinarkkiniyar, Chennai: South India Saiva Siddhanta Works Publishing Society.

Kur̲untogai, 1955, Edited with a commentary by P.V. Somasundaranar, Chennai: South India Saiva Siddhanta Works Publishing Society.

Nar̲r̲iṇai, 1962, Edited with a commentary by A. Narayanaswamy Aiyar, Chennai: South India Saiva Siddhanta Works Publishing Society.

Patir̲r̲uppattu, 1973 (Rpt.), Edited with a commentary by Avvai Duraisamy Pillai, Chennai: South India Saiva Siddhanta Works Publishing Society.

Puranāṉūr̲u, 1978 (Rpt.), Edited with a commentary by P.V. Somasundaranar, Chennai: South India Saiva Siddhanta Works Publishing Society.

Tolkāppiyam–Poruḷ Adigāram, 1982 (Rpt.), With a commentary by Ilampuranar, Chennai: South India Saiva Siddhanta Works Publishing Society.

Tamil̲ Sources (Secondary)

Muthurangam, V., 2009, *Pudiya Uḷaviyal* (in Tamil̲), Puduvai: Ganga Patippakam.

Sivaraj, Dr. D., 1994, *Saṅga Ilakkiyattil Uḷaviyal* (in Tamil̲), Vellore: Sivam Patippakam.

English Sources (Secondary)

Hart, III, George L., 1979, *Poets of the Tamil Anthologies,* New Jersey: Princeton University Press.

Manavalan, Dr. A.A., 2007, *Porulatikararm of Tolkappiyam: An English Version*, Chennai: International Institute of Tamil̲ Studies.

Pandya, Sunil K., 2013 (Ist Ed. 1997), *Human Behaviour*, New Delhi: National Book Trust, India.

Ramanujan, A.K., 1985, *Poems of Love and War*, Delhi: Oxford University Press.

Thangappa, M.L., 2010, *Love Stands Alone – Selections from Tamil Sangam Poetry*, New Delhi: Penguin/ Viking.

Other Sources (Newspaper)

The Times of India, *The Speaking Tree*, 'When The Mind Becomes A Battlefield', A column by Anup Taneja, Delhi Edition, Dated 13th November 2014.

The Times of India, *Speaking Tree*, 'We Need To Rehabilitate The 'Dark' Mind', A column by Pulkit Sharma, Delhi Edition, Dated 16th Jan. 2015.

Other Sources (Websites)

http://Sangamtranslationsbyvaidehi.com

http://www.koodal.com/youth/history/biography.asp?id=71&content= Tamil&name=sigmund-freud

http://webcache.googleusercontent.com/search?q=cache:http://yasskky. blogspot.com/2012/02/blog-post_525.html

http://www.srmuniv.ac.in/Tamilperayam/Tamil_courses/Lessons/MA_ Tamil/IV_Year/matt18/html/mat18005uap1.htm

http://Tamilparks.50webs.com/Tamilpoem/ulaveeyal_paramasivam.html

https://www.indiacurrents.com/articles/2011/12/14/three-guṇas

http://www.speakingtree.in/spiritual-slideshow/seekers/philosophy/who-is-satvik-rajasik-tamasik-person/84876

http://mhcd7.wordpress.com/2013/04/28/உளவியல்-நோக்கில்-காதல்/

Index

About the Author

Govindaswamy Rajagopal (b. 1960 –) is a Professor who teaches Tamil and Comparative Indian Literature in the Department of Modern Indian Languages and Literary Studies at the University of Delhi since 1987 and served as the Head of the Department for three years (2017–2020). He earned his PhD by critically analysing the structure of *mudal* (the "basic elements"), *karu* (the "native elements") and *uri* (the "love themes") in *Akanāṉūṟu* under the guidance of eminence Tamil scholars, Prof. Tamiḻaṇṇal (Rama. Periya Karuppan) and Prof. Pon. Sourirajan. He has also served as the Visiting Professor of Tamil in the Department of Indology, Institute of Oriental Studies, Jagiellonian University, Krakow, Poland for two academic years (2011–2013) and as the Programme External Examiner for Bachelor of Arts in Tamil Language and Literature programme for the Singapore University of Social Sciences (SUSS), Singapore for three academic years (2017–2020).

Besides this book, Rajagopal has authored four books in English titled *Beyond Bhakti: Steps Ahead...* (2007), *Cultural Poetics and Sangam Poetry* (2016), *Etiquette and Ethos: Ethics in Tirukkuṟaḷ and Ācārakkōvai* (2016) and *Re-reading of Classical Tamil Literary Works: Chronicles of Ancient Tamils' Life* (2021) and one book in Tamil titled *Kāmaṉ Kadaippāḍal: Ōr Āyvu* ("The Ballad on Kama: A Study"), (1986). He has presented nearly fifty research papers on various themes at National and International Conferences held in Malaysia, Poland, Czech, France and the USA. Various reputed Research Institutions and Universities in India and abroad have published his research papers focused on Sangam, Tirukkuṟaḷ, and Bhakti literature.

9 789367 000441